MORE

JOYFULLY FULFILLING LIFE

TOM EGGEBRECHT

Cover design by Megan Phillips

Cover photo by Mikaela Hamilton

Interior design and typesetting by Inkwell Creative

ISBN 978-0-692-75730-7

10 9 8 7 6 5 4 3 2 1

DEDICATION

For Tammy, Ashlyn and Ben,
who inspire me daily with unparalleled encouragement and support

Contents

Introduction

WHAT DOES BEING FULLY and creatively alive mean, you ask? To me it means living out your total potential and doing it with uniqueness and flair. In my book, being fully and creatively alive is the only way to live. For as long as I can remember I was encouraged by my parents to chase after creative pursuits. I took piano lessons for four years, and battled my mother all the way through them. I picked up a guitar and took some lessons, but never really got good at it. I loved buying new crayons and watercolors every year just before school started, but always thought that other kids were better artists.

It wasn't until I recognized that I could sing that I began to feel as though I might truly be good at something artistic, something creative. When it came to music class, my third grade teacher was harder on me than any of the other kids. She saw a gift in me, and I knew it. I sang louder and with more fervor than anyone else.

Then my dad, a director of college plays and musicals, began to cast me in his productions. At a tender young age I felt fully and creatively alive. When I stood on the stage and drew a laugh or bowed to applause, I didn't think there could be any better feeling in life. Nearly every year I was in one production or another. The whole process was a blast. I loved memorizing lines, learning the blocking, falling hopelessly in love with my college-aged costars, staying out late on school nights for rehearsal, performing in front of packed houses, and getting to skip school the Monday after the curtain had fallen on the final production.

Thinking back on it now, I probably should have considered it as a career. Being on stage made me feel fully and creatively alive.

When I finished high school, I didn't quite know what I wanted to do with my life, so my parents allowed me to audition for what, in those days, was called a "contemporary Christian band." It was an opportunity to be lead singer in a group that traveled all over the nation, presenting concerts most every night of the week, and frequently performing in a children's musical during the day. For eleven months I felt like I was living the dream (except for the fact that we had to be our own roadies). I got to travel, see the country from the inside of a bus and the insides of peoples' homes, sing in front of audiences, and even meet my future wife.

But I knew that it would all come to an end. I knew that it was only a one-year diversion before I had to face reality, go to college, and figure out which sensible career to pursue. Although my parents always encouraged my creative pursuits, they made it pretty clear that they were to be an avocation, not a vocation. I don't blame them at all. They came out of the sensible fifties and sixties when a steady job was a thing to be valued, and people didn't switch careers as much as they do today.

So I did my duty, went to college (all the while performing in plays and musicals, and playing in Christian rock bands), switching from one major to another, not really sure what I wanted to do with my life. By the time I graduated I thought I wanted to get into Public Relations and work for arts groups, so that I could at least have one foot in the creative scene. But in those days we didn't have internships like students do today, and every job I wanted to apply for had a requirement of at least two years of experience.

In the meantime I got involved with leading the youth group at my church and thought that I might be able to use my love for creativity in the church. So I applied for the seminary, got accepted, moved to St. Louis, and started down the path to becoming a pastor. For four years

I was so wrapped up in my studies that most all other creative pursuits went by the wayside.

As I made my way into the ministry, I dutifully played by the rules and didn't rock the boat. I worked as I had been trained and did it all by the book. The earlier years of my ministry were carried out with blinders on, thinking that everything had to be done the way my seminary professors said they had to be.

But once my feet were wet and I settled into the longest pastorate of my ministry, I began to get restless thinking that a little creativity might draw more people, might bring freshness to the message, might renew my own vigor and bring energy to those that may have felt a bit tired in their own faith walk and life. So when my congregation granted me a sabbatical after seventeen years of ministry, I traveled the country learning from those who were using creativity in their vocations. My eyes were opened wide by those who did things I didn't think I could ever do at my church or in my church body.

When my three months of sabbatical were finished, I came back raring and ready to go with creative techniques, less than traditional thoughts about preaching, and a strong desire to do things in church that would grab the attention of the people in the pews. During my sabbatical I had changed. The people in the pews had not. The creative things I did were met with acceptance in some corners, but in other corners they were denounced. Some weren't ready for visuals, and videos, and stepping outside of the pulpit both literally and figuratively.

The techniques I used were mild compared to the things I had seen on my sabbatical. I was frustrated that I always had to limit myself and think small instead of thinking big. I felt limited by always having to worry about what people were going to think and how my techniques might be a distraction to their faith instead of enhancing it. Creativity can be pursued and carried out, but it doesn't come without a cost. People might not be happy with you. You might not have an income for a time. You might have setbacks. That's part of the creativity terrain.

It was at about the time I went on my sabbatical that our son moved to Nashville and began to pursue his passion of writing and creating music. I saw there in Nashville a whole community of young people who very early in life envisioned their dream, pursued it, and began entrepreneurial pursuits in the creative field. Their stories fascinated me. I was curious about how they made the leap, what it took to get started, what their dreams, goals, and passions were, and whether they felt as though they have already accomplished them. I was interested in what their failures and setbacks taught them, and what advice they would give to others on the same path.

You will find some of their stories in this book. It's my hope that when you read them, you will be encouraged to feel fully alive in the creative pursuit. As you hear from these people, you will see that there is always an artistic alternative in life, and it very often leads to one's own joy while at the same time being helpful to others.

Learning these stories and listening to these people has become my creative outlet as I continue to try and bring creativity into the mainstream of my church body. Whatever your source of creativity is, there are people right now who are using those same tools and who are successfully fulfilling their dreams in a way that makes them feel fully and creatively alive. I hope this book encourages you to do the same in whatever dream you have set your sights on personally or professionally and gives you guidance on how to do that in your particular station in life.

ART NOT ONLY CHANGES THE RECIPIENT, BUT IT CHANGES THE ONE MAKING THE ART.

ONE

Fully Alive

IT HAPPENS FAR MORE often than you may think. People are getting up for work in the morning absolutely amazed at what they get to do every day. They have found a place where their passions and skills intersect. They have discovered that it really is possible to live a life that includes dreams on the way toward being fulfilled. They are doing things they actually like to do. They are learning new skills and artistry along the way. All the while they are helping other people, discovering the incredible value of their own work, and feeling more alive than they would have ever imagined.

These people have seen a fork in the road that leads to creativity, followed after it, and never looked back. They have found a niche that fills a need. People appreciate their work and, in many cases, pay for it. Some are greatly surprised that they have found themselves in this position. But when they think about it, they realize that it took time, work, and effort to get to the place where they feel fully alive.

Have you ever felt as though there was more to life than the way you're living it right now? There are people just like you who have discovered what it means to be fully and creatively alive. They are finding fulfillment in ways many thought they never would. They are living life amazed that they get to get up every day and do what they love to do.

Tanner uses spoken-word poetry to get a message across. Megan is designing hip (and modest) clothing for women. Morgan creates one-of-a-kind pottery. Mikaela discovered a gift for photography. Claire is a comedian who rides the waves of social media. Riley is a sound engineer who has traveled all over the world. Lauren calls herself a visual storyteller. Judson is a graphic designer who dreams of branding upscale food products. Emily makes jewelry and teaches women in Honduras how to start their own self-sustaining jewelry businesses. Patrick tells stories with his photos. Larry has created a business built around his love of live music. Cadence is a brilliant writer who also presents storybook dinners for strangers who come together to get to know one another. Daniel uses his business skills to serve artists who don't have such skills, while exploring his city from the seat of his bicycle.

JORDAN DUNCAN, WARDROBE STYLIST

Jordan Duncan is a wardrobe stylist for musicians and other artists. Her work is seen on album covers, promotional shots, and music videos. Like many other young entrepreneurs, she found her personal calling almost by accident. She had been working for an established fashion company where she designed a leather clutch. Jordan was so proud of the results that she wanted to do a photo shoot. So she pulled together a group of her talented friends to make it all happen. It was an all-day event that included different setups, organizing chaos and managing all the people who had come together for this project.

As she was doing this impromptu project, Jordan discovered a sense of fulfillment she never really felt before. The only way she could describe it was by saying she felt "really alive." So after the shoot she started helping out some photographer friends. Other people allowed her to style them for fun. Pretty soon people were paying Jordan to do something she couldn't believe earned her an income. When asked how she would define what it means to feel "really alive," Jordan says, "It means that I'm being fulfilled in every aspect of the work I'm doing: the creative, relational, and organizational parts. It means that I'm good at it, I love it, and I'm 100% fulfilled when I do my work."

But for Jordan, being really, fully alive doesn't stop there. Jordan is only truly fulfilled when she's doing the same for others. "I want to make a lot of people look nice and feel confident in their lives while at the same time I'm investing in the people around me. I want to be able to choose what is going to be good for me and good for the other person involved in my work. I believe that's how you accomplish things you're really proud of."

U2 LIVES LIFE FULLY ALIVE

I've had moments when I've felt fully alive. Have you? I imagine the band U2 does. I was at one of their concerts a few years ago. It was in Chicago's Soldier Field where I was surrounded by thousands of their other fans. If you've ever been to one of U2's concerts, you know that when the band is on the stage they're definitely "in the zone." They know that their success comes from their fans, and they put on a show that makes every ticket each person buys worth every penny. They don't simply go through the motions. They put their full being into every song, into all of the technological marvel, and into their skilled musicianship. If you asked Bono whether he felt fully alive during any one of their many concerts, I'd be surprised if he'd say he didn't. It's almost as if Bono was born to do what he does for a very well-compensated living.

In fact, In the song, "Magnificent," Bono sings:

I was born, I was born to sing for you
I didn't have a choice but to lift you up
And sing whatever song you wanted me to
I give you back my voice from the womb
My first cry, it was a joyful noise, oh, oh

The beautiful thing about all this is that Bono and his bandmates have provided for me moments when I have felt fully alive simply by being at one of their shows. Being around other people who are living life "fully alive" is infectious. It leads to a common experience. It leads to new friendships. It breaks down walls and barriers. U2 fans are a tribe that for any given concert day put all other differences aside and find themselves united as one.

There was one surreal "fully alive" moment for me in the middle of the Soldier Field show. My wife, Tammy, our son, Ben, and our friend, John, all had General Admission tickets. So we dutifully woke up at 4 a.m., got in line, and waited all day in the heat to gain a coveted place "inside the circle." On the U2360 Tour the stage was set up so that a few hundred lucky fans were able to stand inside the part of the platform that was shaped like a circle. Bono and the whole band used the circle-shaped platform to interact with the audience throughout much of the show.

We were lucky to be among those who stood inside that circle. A high point of the concert came when U2 was doing their joyful anthem, "Beautiful Day." While they were playing the song, I realized there was no place else I would rather be at that very moment. I took a moment to do my own 360 and take in the entire crowd, almost from Bono's vantage point. As I slowly spun around, I couldn't help but notice the pure unadulterated joy on the face of every fan I could see. We were bound together in an unparalleled moment of ecstasy. In that moment it felt like we were all fully alive.

It's hard to explain the feeling, but you know it when it happens. The cares of life disappear. Worry goes away. A sense of true happiness washes right over you. Time stands still.

A friend of mine who played Division 1 college basketball knows what that's like every time she steps foot on the court. She says, "There aren't too many places I can go and just forget about everything, but the basketball court continues to be one of those places. I will always be thankful for that." She has followed her passion and is now an assistant coach for the NYU women's basketball team.

THINK BIG. START SMALL. KEEP GOING.

Uber blogger and marketer Seth Godin, author of many bestsellers including *Linchpin*, says in that book that art "isn't only a painting. Art is anything that's creative, passionate and personal. And great art resonates with the viewer, not only with the creator ... Art is a personal gift that changes the recipient. The medium doesn't matter. The intent does ... Art is a personal act of courage, something one human does that creates change in another."

I would add to Seth's definition of art by saying that art not only changes the recipient, but it changes the one making the art. Art changes others, and it changes the artist. It brings the benefits of growing in courage, in the ability to take risk, in delving into uncomfortable areas. Art changes the artist by making her more aware and thoughtful of everyday items, tasks or events. Art changes the artist by opening his eyes to the beauty in the mundane and the spectacular in the ordinary. I have found this to be the case ever since I devoted myself to writing a blog three times a week. It has made me far more aware of the things happening in my life than I have been ever before. It has made me more contemplative and more thoughtful. In short, it has changed me.

"ART IS A PERSONAL ACT OF COURAGE."

- SETH GODIN

No matter who you are, where you live or what you do, there is always an artistic alternative in life for you. The people in this book have discovered their "art" and have converted it into their daily work. They are finding that what they do not only brings joy into their own lives, but it is also helpful to others, and creates change. At the intersection of engaging in your own true art and providing for the needs of others is a place where purpose and passion collide to make a person feel fully alive.

You are about to meet people who do the things you may have dreamed you could do. They are fully and creatively alive. They would admit that things are not always easy. They would admit that time doesn't *always* fly. They would admit that there are challenges, setbacks, and mistakes. They would tell you that the creative, entrepreneurial life isn't easy. It's hard work.

But they would also tell you that it's incredibly fulfilling to do for a living something that comes naturally. They would tell you how rewarding it is to help other people. They would tell you that though they've worked harder than they ever have before, they wouldn't trade it for anything. They would tell you that they sometimes have to pinch themselves to see if what they are doing is a dream, or whether it is reality.

I'm certain that they would tell you to try it for yourself. They would tell you that you should discover your own personal art that creates change in the recipient as well as change in yourself, and begin to learn how you can be paid to do what it is that you love. They would tell you to start yesterday. If you didn't start yesterday, start today. They would tell you that you will never work harder, nor will you ever feel more fully and creatively alive than when you're standing at the crossroads of your passions and skills.

Charles Lee, CEO and Chief Idea Maker at Ideation Consultancy, Inc., puts it like this: "Think big. Start small. Keep going." Charles is an expert at helping people make their good ideas happen. He has built a business doing what he loves, where his passions and skills intersect. He is doing what makes him feel fully and creatively alive while at the same time helping other people.

So I say to you now in your quest to be fully and creatively alive in whatever dream you wish to pursue: Think big! If it is a business idea, what does your venture look like, fully-grown and fully-functioning? Take some time to think about it.

- ► Write thoughts down.

- ► Make some drawings.

- ► Be specific about where you will work, what you will do, who your customer will be, what your source of revenue will be and even what the name for your company or pursuit will be.

- ► If your goal is more general in nature, follow similar steps to envision what your ideal life would look like. At the same time, start small: What are the smallest steps you can take toward making your Big Thinking a reality?

- ► Map out a week's worth of things you can do each day.

- ► Then do them.

- ► Make a prototype.

- ► Interview others who are doing what you'd like to do.

- ► Set attainable and measurable goals. Keep going: Don't let a day go by without doing at least one small thing that will help you move toward your ultimate goal.

- ► Use free time, early morning, or late night hours.

- ► Have someone else hold you accountable.

- ► Don't stop.

- ► Really, keep going until you've achieved your written goals.

- ► Then set new ones and start all over again.

Think big. Start small. Keep going.

Before you know it, you'll take a look back and be surprised at all the ground you've covered. You will start to feel fully alive. And if you're wondering where you'll tap into all the creativity that's going to make this happen, don't try to conjure it up on your own. There's Someone who can help you with that.

CREATIVE HELP

1   What does a life that's fully and creatively alive specifically look like to you?

2   What is the first step for you to take in order to make that kind of life come alive?

3   Who will hold you accountable as you take your first steps?

THE SENTENCES OF LIFE GIVE YOU A
FILL-IN-THE-BLANK EVERY NOW AND THEN.

TWO

God, the Creative

MORGAN WILLIAMSON, THE POTTER

MORGAN WILLIAMSON MAKES THINGS out of clay. She is an artist that has started a business called Handmade Studio. It all began when she moved to Atlanta for three months while her husband finished school. He suggested that it might be a good time to explore pottery as a medium. It just so happened that her aunt who lived there in Atlanta was in the market for some new dinner plates. So Morgan bought a kiln from a seller on Craigslist, made some plates and even began teaching a pottery class to all the housewives in the neighborhood. They had a big event at the end of the class where she showcased her students' pieces and sold some of her own work.

She thought that was the end of it. But it wasn't. Far from it. After giving it up for a while she felt a void that simply couldn't be filled. So she bought another kiln, made a home studio and started creating more ceramic pieces. She built a brand and a following using social media. One day she turned around and said, "Oh my gosh! This is a business!"

But it's really so much more than that. Morgan says, "I'm passionate about art, people, and God, and I feel like my work encompasses all those things. Scripture is filled with references about clay and a potter. I get to create something that originated in God. Being able to participate in that is very special in my mind."

Morgan gets a bit introspective when she thinks about the little spoons she makes. "I make tiny little ceramic spoons. I think about how much I *love* those spoons. Each one is a perfect little spoon. They have just as much value to me as a huge, ornate serving piece. Things like that made out of clay remind me of, and point back to, God and how he views us and his children and how we're all his children and how each one is precious in his eyes."

THE CREATIVITY OF THE CREATIVE GOD

At the beginning of all things, Scripture tells us, God created the heavens and the earth. He did it by simply speaking all things into existence. That is, until he made the crown of his creation: human beings. When God created Adam and Eve he did more than speak them into existence. He formed them from the dust of the ground. Like an artist using clay, God lovingly formed his most beloved creatures, paying attention to every detail.

Look around you. No two people are alike. Each one of us is unique. We have creativity built right into us.

The nine grandchildren of my parents are a great example of the variety and creativity with which we are made, and the variety of creativity we are given:

> ▶ Natalie just finished working for Boeing so that she could be a full-time mom to her little girl, Brecken, and now a pair of twins. She is a runner, an accomplished food-blogger and a fantastic baker and cook.

- ▶ Julia is a nurse who works part time in the NICU, and also stays at home to take care of her two sons. She played college basketball, loves to read and is a huge Aaron Rodgers and Green Bay Packers fan.

- ▶ Ashlyn graduated from college with a degree in theatre and lives in Orlando, Florida, with her new husband, where she works in the entertainment department at Sea World and takes on an occasional acting gig.

- ▶ Ben is a singer/songwriter who lives in Nashville, where he spends most every day writing, recording, or doing all he can to move his career forward.

- ▶ Quinn was a high-energy college basketball player who now works in the insurance industry, considers theology in his free time, and expresses his opinion of his dearly loved Green Bay Packers (are you sensing a theme in this family?).

- ▶ Madi studied history in college and was able to do an internship at the Smithsonian Institution in Washington, D.C. She'd love to be a museum curator.

- ▶ Renatta is studying English and is thinking about becoming an attorney. She has the most sarcastic wit of most anyone I know.

- ▶ Clayton is in college, where he plays basketball and studies sports management. He collects basketball shoes (of all things).

- ▶ Libby is a high school runner, dancer, fashionista, a wonderfully creative photographer, and a girl with a heart bigger than most kids her age.

God's creativity is abundantly evident in the stars at night and in the morning blooms. I recently got an app on my phone that allows me to point my phone to the sky, and it identifies all the stars, planets and constellations. It even shows me some stars that are barely visible to the naked eye. I've learned that some of the stars I see are larger than our sun and earth combined. How could those come into existence without the intelligence of a God who is the source of all creativity?

Every morning I see the flowers on our porch stretch toward the light so that they can generate energy through photosynthesis. Somehow those flowers know the direction of light so that they can create oxygen as efficiently as possible. And no two of those flowers are alike. They are uniquely painted with various colors and designs, and structured with different-shaped leaves and stems of various lengths.

Jesus said, "See how the lilies of the field grow. They do not labor or spin. Yet I tell you that not even Solomon in all his splendor was dressed like one of these. If that is how God clothes the grass of the field, which is here today and tomorrow is thrown into the fire, will he not much more clothe you, O you of little faith?" (Matthew 6:28b-30, NIV).

Think about it. You are a human being. As such, you are the most intelligent, most thoughtful, most emotional of all of God's creatures. You are clothed with the colors of creation. God created and designed you to be superior to everything else he made. With that kind of creativity going into your design, you are created to be creative. You are instilled with creativity. You are more creative than you ever knew or thought you could be. Yes, you.

When I was in high school I was asked to write something for a publication that the school was putting out. I thought, "There's no way *I* could ever do that. I just don't have that kind of skill." When I mentioned the assignment to my dad, he said, "You should have no problem with that. You're a very creative person. All you kids are." Though I had been involved in creative pursuits already much of my life, it never dawned on me until that moment that I was created to be creative. I wrote the piece and it was well received. I never again doubted that I had creativity built right into me. All it took was for someone to affirm it.

The same is true for you. I promise you that if you dig down deeply enough, you will find a creative spark in there somewhere. Stephen Schwartz got it exactly right when he wrote the musical *Children of Eden*. He put these words into the mouth of Eve, the first woman ever created:

The spark of creation is flickering within me
The spark of creation is blazing in my blood
A bit of the fire that lit up the stars
And breathed life into the mud, the first inspiration
The spark of creation

I see a mountain and I want to climb it
I see a river and I want to leave shore
Where there was nothing let there be something, something made by me
There's things waiting for me to invent them
There's worlds waiting for me to explore
I am an echo of the eternal cry of
Let there be!

MIKAELA HAMILTON, THE PHOTOGRAPHER

Mikaela Hamilton discovered the spark of creation within her. She grew up focusing on athletics, and was an avid soccer player. Throughout most of her young life she was a "closet creative." She always had an interest in creative pursuits, but never thought she'd be able to chase after them. Mikaela always found herself boxed into the "athlete category."

She intended to go to college to play soccer, but injured her knee. Beside that, she was burned out on soccer, but didn't want to admit it to herself. Since she was no longer going to play soccer, she found herself at school with an abundant amount of free time. The knee surgery had removed from her everything she had known. Her family wasn't around, and she was surrounded by people who knew nothing about her.

Life had given her a "fill-in-the-blank." She figured she could discover a whole new outlet for herself. She asked for a camera for her 20th birthday, and with it went to the Dominican Republic on a spring break with a group from her school. It was there that she discovered just how she was going to fill in the blank of her life.

In the Dominican Republic she volunteered at an elementary school.

There was a little boy in the school named Sam, who had striking hazel eyes. She snapped a picture of him, looked at it, and thought, "I really like this whole photo thing." She went back to school and started shooting anything she could get in front of her camera: marriage proposals, sorority houses, weddings—anything she could possibly put into the form of digital print.

This all led to her getting a job at the university she attended with the school's Department of Technology and Design. Mikaela started to learn the technical side of photography with the equipment she was able to access in that department. She stopped shooting everything on the automatic setting, and learned about light and exposure.

"I GET TO CREATE SOMETHING THAT ORIGINATED IN GOD."

- MORGAN WILLIAMSON

There are times when our life stories have no passion or zing. Maybe you are there right now. But the sentences of life give you a "fill-in-the-blank" every now and then. Those are the moments when you have the opportunity to discover the creativity that the Creator God has placed within you. Don't compare yourself to others and the way they fill out their creative pursuits. Find your own creativity. Dig deep down and determine what makes *your* heart sing. What is it that makes time fly by when you are doing it? Are there creative things you once did, perhaps as a child, that are now but a distant memory? How can you recover them? What steps will you take to affirm the creativity God has placed within you?

Fill in the blanks of life with something that you've always wanted to do but never had the time. *Make* the time. Fill in that time with incremental pursuits of a passion you've always had. Fill in the blank with photography, or art, or writing, or crafting, or mixing, or shaping. Fill it in with color, light, and flair.

And pray. Since prayer includes listening to God, you will discover that petitioning the Almighty Creator for inspiration and creative insight will bring renewed energy, interesting ideas, and the desire to follow through. Communication with the Author of the universe is certain to turn the spark of creativity into a flame that will grow and light up your life with fulfilling pursuits and new ideas for how to share them.

You will discover that the creativity implanted in you by God can be taught, and learned, and practiced. The full-grown, full-blown art that is produced doesn't necessarily come without some blood, sweat, and tears. But the spark is there, the desire is there and you may have even found that others have affirmed that gift in you, whatever it may be. So take lessons. Learn skills. Practice early in the morning or late at night. You will see the creative hand of God actively at work in the creative output you begin to share.

Whenever you are feeling blah and not creative, not fulfilled and like you are not accomplishing things, keep an eye out for those sentences in life that provide a wonderfully unexpected "fill-in-the-blank." The creativity of the Creator God is part of your DNA. Discover it, use it and fill it in. Trust that the God who created you will create *through* you.

CREATIVE HELP

1 What is the art or creativity God has planted in you?

2 How can you renew an artistic pursuit that you once enjoyed?

3 Where is the time that you are now wasting that could be utilized to pursue your creativity?

WHEN YOU'RE DOING SOMETHING YOU
REALLY LIKE, YOU WON'T BE AFRAID
TO EXPERIMENT AND GIVE THINGS A
TRY EVEN IF IT MEANS FAILURE.

THREE

Do What You Like

CLAIRE LINIC, THE COMEDIAN

BE FOREWARNED. IF YOU find yourself around Claire Linic, you're going to laugh. I met Claire when she was in college. Every time I was in her presence I laughed. Hard. Even if she didn't know it at the time, Claire was destined to become a comedienne. Already then I could picture her as one of the comedic actors on *Saturday Night Live*.

Claire has the gift of taking the things that happen in everyday life and turning them into a joke. Her jokes come out of her mouth as fast as they go through her head. She's as quick-witted as they come.

Almost on a whim, upon graduation Claire decided to move to Chicago and study at the famed *The Second City*. It changed her life. Before she started her classes she felt as if she had very little focus. But the instructors and classes at *The Second City* gave her a running start in the business. Now Claire uses Tumblr and Twitter and social media of all kinds to tell stories and produce comedy.

Along with a friend of hers, she created a franchise called *The*

Awkward Phase which has become a live stage show and is now also a book. *The Awkward Phase* is all about telling the stories we all have in those 'tween, middle school years. In the live stage show six people get eight minutes to tell their "awkward phase" stories in whatever way they want. Some sing, some dance, one woman dyed her hair on stage, some even repeat childhood talent show acts. Claire says that 70% of it is very funny, but some of it is a "tear fest." She says that it's almost uncanny how a theme seems to crop up at every live stage show.

Claire and her husband, Alan, have also started a Twitter account called @wefoughtabout. They post the things they, well, fight about, and the results are hilarious. "Claire laughed at me for crying during *The Voice*." "I told Alan my contacts were dry and he blew in my eyes." "I walked in front of the TV while Claire was playing a video game." "Alan said I wasn't fiercely independent." The Twitter feed drew the attention of the national media. The CBS television network bought their postings and wanted to see of they could make them into a sitcom. The problem was, CBS decided that you couldn't do a full show based on conflict with a character who is "very sweet with a short fuse, but completely crazy."

Claire's favorite type of performance is improv. She likes it because it's one of the only kinds of comedy that's a team effort. She has found the Chicago comedy community to be very tight-knit and a rousing base for improvisation all over the city. It's a team in and of itself.

Claire says, "I took one class at *The Second City* and everything clicked. Improv clicked for me. I did improv in my mind for twenty-plus years and didn't know where to apply it. This is something I can actually be good at." Claire is a prime example of someone who lives out one of the most important keys to the success of any creative pursuit—do what you like.

She says, "Put your head down and do what you like. If you're trying to do something simply for status, it won't get noticed. When *I'm* passionate about something, it makes others passionate about it as well. Create something because *you* like it, not because you think others will like it. That's where a lot of my failure has come from ... being the kind of performer I thought I was supposed to be. If you're doing something just to get noticed, people can feel that. It has a certain smell to it. If something affects *your* life or has a personal meaning to *you*, it's got a whole different smell to it."

When you're doing something you really like, you won't be afraid to experiment and give things a try even if it means failure. Claire says that she's failed "brilliantly." She says, "I've failed more times than I've succeeded. I've

"PUT YOUR HEAD DOWN AND DO WHAT YOU LIKE."

- CLAIRE LINIC

got a thicker skin than I used to have. For every article I publish online there are three or four more I've written that were never published, and those are some of my favorite articles. Half of the books I've pitched will never come to fruition." Failure is never something to be afraid of in a creative pursuit, nor is it ever something that should derail you in your quest for your goal.

TRAVELING THE WORLD AND TEACHING OTHERS

Chris Guillebeau, *New York Times* and *Wall Street Journal* bestselling author, likes to travel. He had the goal of visiting every country in the world by the time he was thirty-five. So he found a way to do what he liked and get paid for it. He accomplished his goal on April 4, 2013, when he visited Norway. Along the way he found time to write a blog, author three books and teach others to live lives and do work that they loved. While he's traveling, writing and teaching others to do the same, he's also giving back. A portion of the profits from his book, *The Art of Non-Conformity*, go to Charity: Water, a non-profit organization bringing clean and safe drinking water to people in developing nations.

That book has the subtitle: "Set your own rules, live the life you want, and change the world." That's what Chris is doing. But he's also helping others do the same. He set up an online course called "Make Your Dream Trip a Reality." It is a thirty-day video-based course that guarantees two free plane tickets and at least three free nights in a hotel by the time each student finishes the class. (Take the class and find out for yourself.)

If you follow his Instagram feed (@193countries), you can tell that Chris is doing what he likes. It's hard to keep up with his globetrotting. One night he'll be posting the picture of a bourbon Manhattan in Hong Kong and before you know it he'll post a picture of a cup of coffee in Australia. Though he has achieved his goal of visiting every country in the world, Chris loves what he is doing so much that he simply can't stop. He's still traveling all over the world.

He's even happy to tell you how to start your own quest to do what you like. *The $100 Startup* helps readers to "reinvent the way you make a living, do what you love, and create a new future." Chris calls it the "follow-your-passion" model. He believes that the most successful small businesses are those that are based on a personal hobby or interest of the founder.

His advice is to focus "relentlessly on the point of convergence between what you love to do and what other people are willing to pay for." Claire does what she likes to do. She has a constant improv show going on in her mind. Now she writes, performs, and does videos that make people laugh. And people are willing to pay for it. Chris does what he likes to do. He travels all over the world and teaches others how to travel nearly for free. And people are willing to pay for it.

DOING WHAT YOU LIKE BRINGS SUSTAINABILITY

Think of people who are doing what they like to do. Does it seem that they tend to work harder than someone who doesn't particularly enjoy what they are doing? You've heard the old saying: Do what you love and you'll never work another day in your life. Nothing could be further from the truth. When people do what they like to do, they often work harder than perhaps they ever have in their life.

Two successful writers who like what they do are Jon Acuff and Jeff Goins. Go ahead and Google them to find out everything they're up to. Both have released bestselling books. Acuff is also writing blogs and magazine articles and fulfilling speaking engagements all over the country. Goins writes blogs, as well, but he's making the majority of his income by teaching online classes on writing, building a tribe, and marketing books.

They both work harder than they probably thought they ever would in their lives. Yet they're enjoying every moment of living a life they thought they never would. They recognized their passion and not only pursued it, but worked so hard at it that it became their primary source of income. Now they're working hard just to keep up with all they have begun. They're doing what they like. It's not easy. Yet it's hard work that they enjoy.

Brandon Stanton is the photographer behind the internet sensation Humans of New York (humansofnewyork.com). When Brandon graduated from college, he moved to Chicago and became a bond trader, taking photographs on the weekends. Photography was his real passion, so when he lost his job as a bond trader, he decided to move to New York City and take photographs of people. A Wikipedia article about Stanton claims that his original idea was to photograph 10,000 people in New York and place their portraits on a map of the city. Eventually he began to use a Facebook page as the main means of releasing his work, and soon the portraits were accompanied by captions and quotes.

In an interview with Barbara Benson (crainsnewyork.com), Stanton says, "One of the most interesting parts of Humans of New York is how quickly it took off. I started doing street photography, pictures of people. During the first three years of Humans of New York, I probably took less than 10 days off, and took pictures for six to eight hours a day. I had no friends. I had no money. When I wasn't doing the work, I was thinking about it. You can get lucky. But it is impossible to sustain an audience daily or hold their interest without consistency. In order for an audience to be built, you have to have consistency before you get to your first fan."

It's obviously much easier to sustain something when you really like doing it. If you're going to pursue a passion and really want it to become a money-making venture or career, as Stanton says, you have to have consistency. You cannot give up too easily. Doing what you like is a major step toward being able to overcome the naysayers and the internal trepidation that anyone might feel when taking a leap and venturing into something new. In other words, you'd better do what you like because in order to attain any kind of sustainability you're going to be doing it day in and day out, season after season. So why not enjoy it?

You *can* do what you like. There are any number of things you *like* to do that you could turn into an income-producing job or career. You'd be surprised what those jobs or careers might be. People are making money producing videos they use to teach anything from how to use Scrivener software to how to establish a platform that will help you write, sell, and market books.

In the Internet Age almost anything is possible in terms of creating a career doing what you like to do. But determining just what it is you *like* to do, and how to create an income stream is just the start. The next step is learning more.

CREATIVE HELP

1 If money were no object, what would you most like to do?

2 What have your failures taught you?

3 How can you more consistently do the one thing you really like to do?

PEOPLE WHO ARE FULLY AND CREATIVELY
ALIVE SEE EVERY DAY AS AN OPPORTUNITY
TO LEARN SOMETHING NEW.

FOUR

Always Learn

ONE OF THE KEYS to comedienne Claire's comedy is that she never stops learning. Every day she tries to learn something new. It's the fuel that fires a good improv sketch. Very late one night Claire was on the internet diving down what she calls a "worm hole" researching the difference between a legless lizard and a snake. Did you even know there's such a thing as a legless lizard? I don't even like encountering snakes, much less a "legless lizard." Keep me far, far away.

But that research happened to come in handy just a short time later when Claire found herself in the middle of a scene at an improv club and based a whole character on the difference between a legless lizard and a snake. Don't ask me. I have no idea.

People who go into business for themselves can't afford to stop learning. Ever. The moment they do they risk the chance of becoming irrelevant. Technology, information and knowledge are growing so quickly that if an entrepreneur fails to keep up, she will most certainly be passed up by someone who devotes the time and dedicates the energy toward being a lifelong, day-by-day student.

Learning comes in many shapes and forms. It can be formal or informal. It can be intentional or unintentional. But it means always keeping an eye and an ear open for technology, information, or knowledge that will be beneficial for the bottom line. It means storing away what you learn in an organized way by developing idea storehouse that include such things as Dropbox folders or Evernote files. It means reminding oneself to take the posture of a student each and every day.

RILEY VASQUEZ, FRONT OF HOUSE ENGINEER AND TOUR MANAGER

Riley Vasquez is a Front of House Engineer and Tour Manager. That means he runs the sound for bands and manages all of their money and logistics. He has traveled all over the world doing what he loves. And he is a diehard student. It started when he was young. His family owned retail music stores, so instruments and music were always a part of his life. When he was in elementary school, he learned to play the guitar and piano, and practiced his craft by playing both in church. When the sound guys at church wouldn't show up, Riley learned how to run the sound board.

When he went to college, Riley wanted to play bass for the world-renowned Lee University Campus Choir. Circumstances forced him instead to run the sound for the 96-voice choir and band. He did it for a year and a half and got his first taste of touring life. His desire to learn more about the technical aspect of running sound led him to transfer to another college in Nashville where he began to meet people in the music business. He found himself in the right place at the right time, putting on a good attitude every day even though his university taught him at first that he was the lowest of the low and had to earn his stripes in the music business.

The crucial moment came a few years later when a friend of his called and asked if he wanted to run sound for their band at a show in Atlanta. The pay would be $50.00. He quit his job at Cracker Barrel and immediately drove to Atlanta for the show.

Six months later the band's manager asked him to be their Tour Manager and Front of House sound person for the band's tour. He didn't even know what that meant. So he went to his school books and looked up "Tour Manager," looked at Wikipedia, and did all kinds of research before saying, "Yeah, sure, I'll do it." He went on the tour which led to numerous of opportunities for him. Now he's been on tours that have taken him to Australia, Europe and Mexico. He's run a show at Universal Studios and afterwards got a VIP tour.

But that certainly doesn't mean he has stopped learning. Riley wants to do more. He'd like to take on bigger tours. He's thinking about starting his own tech company. He's considering where his work in the music industry might take him. His attitude of lifelong learning has taken him down the path of talking to people who are successful in the music and tech industry.

He went to San Francisco for a week to meet key people involved in Twitter, Google, GoPro, and Square. The idea was to become friends with as many people as he possibly could in as many different types of tech industries as he could. All he did was ask his friends if they knew anyone in San Francisco, and they connected him to these people. Once the connection was made, he simply reached out with an offer to buy them coffee or beer, and most said yes.

His learning has also come from failure. As he was pursuing the dream of leading the touring life, he had his share of difficulties. Feedback is the worst nightmare and worst enemy of the sound guy. If feedback is heard at an artist's show, they will more than likely not hire you back. Riley's had his share of that ear-piercing noise. There were other times where he miscommunicated as the Tour Manager and the show had some hiccups.

Riley's worst time came when he was working for a national act mixing the sound in the band's monitors and acting as tour manager. "We were doing Summerfest in Milwaukee at a massive stage," he said. "It was my first show on the tour. We flew in on a plane, so all the equipment was supposed to be there when we got there. We showed up at 10 a.m. for our sound check and nothing was there. They told me I didn't order anything. I actually *had* sent in the order, but it didn't get to the right person. I made phone calls and got the equipment delivered, so in the end everything went OK. At a show the very next day computers went down, a crazy storm came from out of nowhere, and everything was going wrong. I was the tour manager and things just weren't going right. I was supposed to go with them on their very next tour, but they called me and fired me."

As a lifelong student, Riley learns just as much from the failures as he does from people in the industry and doing research. When asked about pursuing the prospect of becoming Front of House Engineer and Tour Manager, Riley says, "It's definitely a risk you have to take. Don't be afraid to take a risk. It's understandable to be afraid. Sometimes you just have to quit your day job and take a job for $50.00. Take someone to dinner. Figure out a way to get your foot in the door. You need to be meeting people every day. At some point there's going to be a way in. Doors don't stay open for a long time, so you've got to walk through them quickly."

And keep on learning.

OPPORTUNITIES ABOUND FOR LEARNING SOMETHING NEW

People who are fully and creatively alive see every day as an opportunity to learn something new. They learn about things that may not even have immediate benefit. Being a professional student is a key to being prepared at any moment for opportunities that are presented to entrepreneurial artists.

We have been given a world of learning right at our fingertips. The stroke of a key and sometimes just a few dollars lead to learning opportunities that people in previous generations could have only imagined.

Michael Hyatt (michaelhyatt.com), who calls himself "Your Virtual Mentor," will show you how to build your business or entrepreneurial endeavor in what he calls Platform University. Master Classes in Platform University give you access to successful people like Jeff Goins,

Donald Miller, Dave Ramsey, and Amy Porterfield. They teach you how to write content people want to read, use Facebook to create massive engagement, build a cash-generating email list, and even how to build a powerful brand "through story."

"DON'T BE AFRAID TO TAKE A RISK."

- RILEY VASQUEZ

Platform University lets you peek in as Hyatt does web site makeovers for those who are attempting to build their own brand. The University even has "backstage passes" that show you how Michael does everything from setting up his office to how he creates a podcast.

In days gone by this kind of education would cost time, travel and thousands of dollars. Today anyone can subscribe to an online class and have access to education and information while sitting in a home office or at the kitchen table.

Seth Godin has built his whole career on creating content for internet consumption. He puts out a daily (yes, daily) blog that you an access for free. But he also has more focused content that can be consumed online for a small (and it usually is pretty small) fee. He has used a platform called Udemy.com to teach a class to people who want to be "freelancers." The class will show you how to move up, build assets, manage clients, choose strategies, tell stories, price your work, find your unique voice, organize and connect and turn pro. I purchased the class and it cost me less than $30. What I learned from the class is far superior and far more valuable than anything I could have learned at my local community college, which would have cost me far more time and money.

Udemy.com doesn't just offer Seth Godin classes. It offers a myriad of courses that will help you learn something new every day. You can learn accounting, or Android app development, or even how to create an online course.

If you need a place from which to start *all* of your endeavors, you can go online and find *Creating Your Life Plan*, by Donald Miller. The plan helps you bring clarity and focus to your life, organize and improve your relationships, give you a new attitude when you face challenges, experience a deep sense of meaning, and change yourself and your community for the better. Miller makes it all interesting by interviewing author Shauna Niequist. As she makes her way through the plan, you can see what a positive impact it will have in your life.

There are so many resources available that you could never take advantage of them all. So you'll want to focus your topics, pick a few things at a time to learn and give yourself a timeline to complete them. The best way to do that is to actually schedule learning opportunities into each day or each week. If you currently have a job, you could do your learning in the evening or over lunch hours. If you happen to be looking for a job, or are between jobs, you could make learning your temporary job and use your six- or eight-hour "work day" to watch videos, take notes and complete assignments. You'll be surprised at how much you can learn in just a short amount of time.

Now, I wonder, what *is* the difference between a legless lizard and a snake?

CREATIVE HELP

1 How will you see to it that you learn at least one new thing each day?

2 What risky thing can you produce today?

3 Which online class will you commit to take within the next month?

**CHOOSING TO BE POSITIVE WILL BE
THE FORCE FIELD THAT DISTANCES
YOURSELF FROM NEGATIVITY.**

FIVE

Aim Your Attitude

YOU'VE HEARD THE PHRASE, "It's all about attitude"? It may not be *all* about attitude, but a positive attitude certainly helps when there are failures and setbacks (as there are certain to be as you pursue a passion or chase a dream). Negativity only drains, puts work on the back burner and drives away the very people who might help. Choose your attitude. After all, it *is* a choice.

LAUREN LEDBETTER, BRAND DESIGNER

"Give yourself a lot of grace." That's the advice of Lauren Ledbetter, a freelance "brand designer" who considers herself a visual storyteller. "When you're in it for the first time and you make a decision to start your own business, you're going to fail. All the decisions you have to make—about workspace, how to be productive and all the other little choices you have to make—you can't really know until you fail. The harder we are on ourselves the worse it is. Know that there's a learning curve and give yourself a kind of grace."

Choosing your attitude is a very real approach. All you have to do is look at the "About" page on Lauren's web site to see that she does just that. The positivity just oozes off the screen. Peruse her "talking points" and you can see the attitude she chooses most every day: White is my favorite color // I'm always up for a road trip // Handwritten letters are the key to my heart // Type and perfect kerning are borderline obsessions // I value sincerity // Nashville stole my heart // If you have any vintage turquoise jewelry you don't want, I'll gladly take it // I want to be Tammy Taylor when I grow up // A white farmhouse is the culmination of my dream life // I thrive off of people with enthusiasm // I enjoy gathering people over a meal more than you could even imagine // I'd be forever content with a hammock, a river, and skipping stones // I spend more money on typefaces than clothes // I like to make everything from scratch // Otis Redding on vinyl is usually playing at my house // I purposely linger too long on hugs.

Lauren moved from Seattle to Nashville to go to Belmont University. She started as a Music Business major, but finished school as a Design major. Right out of college she was the Art Director for a small record label. For her it was the perfect marriage between music and design and the fulfillment of her goals to that point. In her mind it was the perfect job. She wanted to create visuals that made sense with the music that the artists were creating. But she began to discover that the label was very "corporate."

As she became more and more disillusioned with her position at the record label, Lauren began to build a base of freelance clients with whom she really wanted to work, who valued branding and gave her a safety net to make mistakes. In this process she created what she calls a "brand workshop" for people to discover what their true brand was.

It wasn't long before she took a leap and started her own business. She says it was "so terrifying, but such a blessing." She immediately chose her attitude. Yes, there was fear. But more importantly she viewed this new opportunity and new chapter in her life as a good thing.

She says, "I was my own guinea pig. I hung around the people I wanted to be working with. People who appreciated my work came along." With an emotional connection to her clients, Lauren became an advocate for the things they were passionate about. She was able to give people the tools to do what they wanted to do.

Lauren's attitude shines through when she talks about her passion. "I'm passionate about people and their stories, and I want to be creative in what I do. I would be terrible in an office job. I love the 'people' element of things. I love being on somebody's team. I love encouraging them. I want to push their expectation of themselves outside of the boundary."

Wouldn't you love to have Lauren on *your* team? You couldn't help but be positive, proactive, and optimistic with her around. Who wouldn't want to have a team member who says, "I love to speak life into other people's dreams"?

If you would love having someone do that for you, just think about how your positive, proactive and optimistic attitude could help others. As you build your platform, start a business, pursue your passion, or chase your dream, consider how choosing that type of attitude every single day will help and benefit your clients or those you serve.

As Lauren reflects on how she wants to grow her business, it continues to be centered on her attitude. "We're our own worst critics. I'm always thinking about what I can do better. But I love digging deeply into other people: how you are wired, you are unique, let's celebrate that. I like to give people the confidence that they need whether it's a logo or a web site. I want to be more on the 'encouragement' side of things. I want to make branding more of a party. I want to get people together and just celebrate the fact

"I LOVE TO SPEAK LIFE INTO OTHER PEOPLE'S DREAMS."

- LAUREN LEDBETTER

that they are unique. It would be great fun. But my goal is to be better at encouraging people and making things happen for people even when they can't see that it's possible. I want to instill confidence in them."

Aiming your attitude means being helpful to yourself, too, and being aware of your own needs. Lauren encourages her clients to figure out when they are most productive and to use that time to its greatest efficiency. At those unproductive times of the day she encourages "me" time. When you know your limits and step away for a while, you become much more healthy and more readily able to pursue your very best work when the creative juices start flowing.

Lauren recognizes this in herself. She says, "When I take on more than I can handle, I get frustrated. I have to know my own limits. When I'm passionate about something I sometimes put myself out on a limb. I've got to know when to stop. I have to realize when my productivity and personal mental health are more important than immediate money. If I take on too much, it bogs me down when I really should have joy in my life."

NEGATE THE NEGATIVE

Beware of the opposite, too, though. Be on the lookout for the ways in which other people's negative attitudes can have an impact on your attitude. Negativity is much more contagious than a good attitude. Have you ever worked with someone whose attitude was always in question? You know how it is. You come into work in the morning always wondering which person you'll be greeting. Will it be the happy-go-lucky cheerful one, or the depressed and dour one?

I once worked with someone like that. It was a person with whom every member of our staff had contact every single day. Even if I didn't encounter this particular staff member, I could always tell what her mood was based on the demeanor of everyone else in the building. If she was in a bad or sad mood, it spread throughout the whole place like an infection. Nobody wants to work with someone like that. Work can sometimes be difficult enough without having to deal with the negative attitude of a coworker, boss or client. Productivity goes down. Creativity wanes. People are wondering what they can do to raise the mood of a particular team member instead of doing good, productive work.

Instead, be the one from whom everyone gets a boost of energy and positivity. For twelve years I had an assistant who had a smile on her face every single day. She could be sicker than a dog and still greet me with a smile. She always had my back no matter the criticisms I received or the fiery arrows that came from any which direction. If I needed a lift, I knew that I could get it just by walking into the office.

Motivational speaker Zig Ziglar, said, "Beautiful things happen when you distance yourself from negativity." The trick is figuring out how to do just that. It begins every morning when you wake up and head to the bathroom. In that short trip you can choose your attitude for the entire day. Before coffee, before breakfast, before even speaking to anyone else, you can consciously choose to be positive. If you need a reminder, put a note on your bathroom mirror to remind yourself: "I choose to be positive today."

Choosing to be positive will be the force field that distances yourself from negativity. Your own attitude will be the shield that deflects the awful attitudes of others that you are certain to encounter most every day. When the day starts on a positive note, beautiful things happen because you don't let the critics get you down. Even if you're feeling less than stellar on the inside, you can choose to *show* a positive attitude by smiling, engaging with people, focusing on the needs of others, asking them how their day is going, or simply being present in a conversation. Beautiful things will most certainly happen that way.

Author Charles Swindoll wrote about the beauty of being able to choose one's own attitude every day: "The longer I live, the more I realize the impact of attitude on life. Attitude, to me, is more important than facts. It is more important than the past, than education, than money, than circumstances, than failures, than successes, than what other people think or say or do. It is more important than appearance, giftedness, or skill. It will make or break a company ... a church ... a home. The remarkable thing is we have a choice every day regarding the attitude we will embrace for that day. We cannot change the inevitable. The only thing we can do is play on the one string we have, and that is our attitude ... I am convinced that life is 10% what happens to me, and

90% how I react to it. And so it is with you ... we are in charge of our attitudes."

So take charge today. Choose to put a smile on your face. Make sure others are impacted by your positive attitude. There are plenty of negative things and negative people in this world. You will stand out when you choose to do this one simple thing every day. People will be drawn to you. Clients will appreciate you. Your creativity will flourish. Your energy will increase. Your goals will be met.

Take a cue from Lauren and "speak life into people's dreams." Even better, take this advice from Lauren's mom: "If you're in a garden and you're only focused on the worms or the weeds, you can't take a step back and see how beautiful the garden is." The garden of this life is beautiful if we just step back and take a look.

In the end, your positive attitude *isn't* all about you. It's about helping and serving others. Lauren and her mom get it. And if you need a little Otis Redding on vinyl playing in your house to make it all happen, go ahead and do it. Choosing your attitude makes a difference that others will notice.

CREATIVE HELP

1 Take note of your attitude right now. If it's less than good, what can you do to choose a better one?

2 Who has an attitude that you'd like to emulate? How can you spend more time with her or him?

3 What reminders will you give yourself to retain a positive attitude?

REVEL IN BEING YOURSELF AND
DON'T BE AFRAID TO BE WEIRD.

SIX

MEGAN PHILLIPS, FASHION DESIGNER

WHEN I THINK OF Megan Phillips, I think of authenticity, uniqueness, and *joie de vivre*. I've known Megan since she was in high school, and have always seen in her a distinctiveness that told me she is a person who has a free and willing spirit. She's comfortable in her own skin. She enjoys being herself, and it shows in the passion she is pursuing. Megan is taking on the big, bold world of fashion and design and is beginning to make her own mark.

Her journey into the fashion industry began when she started at a college in Indiana. In true "Megan" fashion, she left the school after a year because she didn't feel as though it was "risky enough." She wanted to do something bigger. At that point she didn't even know what that "bigger" thing was. She had dreams of living and working in New York City but didn't know how to bridge the gap to get there. So she decided to transfer to Belmont University in Nashville, Tennessee. Since it's mainly a music school in "Music City" she thought she'd like to go into graphic design for musicians. She enjoyed it, but began to learn it really wasn't her thing.

In the middle of that school year she went home to Milwaukee and went out shopping with a friend. In the middle of the H&M clothing store they had a conversation that changed the direction of Megan's life. She admitted to her friend that she really didn't know what career she wanted to pursue or what her dream was. Without missing a beat her friend said, "I always thought you'd do fashion. I always felt like that was you."

The light went on in Megan's head as she realized "style" was always a huge part of her life. She went back to Nashville and tried to figure out how to implement this new idea into her coursework. Belmont didn't have a degree in fashion, so Megan had to pave her own way. That included getting an internship at a company called Rent the Runway, which rents out furniture and name brand, couture outfits for special events. She became the Belmont campus representative for Rent the Runway. The internship taught her lessons in leadership, how to sell fashion, what "connects" with women, marketing tactics, and figuring out a budget.

Along the way she heard about Dream Careers (summerinternships. com), an all-inclusive package providing an internship in the career of your choice and teaching you how to achieve the career of your dreams. She knew her parents really couldn't afford the program, but she asked them anyway, and told them that this would be a very significant way for her to learn whether the fashion industry was what she ought to pursue. Her parents were immediately on board with the idea, and did what they could to make it happen financially.

Megan talked to a representative at Dream Careers and made it clear she wanted an internship in the fashion industry, preferably with a high fashion, designer label. The rep interviewed her, looked over her résumé and determined that the best fit for Megan would be with either Michael Kohrs or Vera Wang. Megan decided that since Vera Wang is so "whimsical and creative" she wanted to send her résumé there. The rep from Dream Careers cautioned that Wang typically takes mostly design students from New York, so Megan wasn't too sure she'd get it. But, lo and behold, within the next month all the pieces fell into place. She was offered an internship at Vera Wang, and was on her way to New York City.

Megan was told that the key to her getting the internship was her work with Rent the Runway. The plan was becoming more clear in her mind. It wasn't long before Megan realized that her experience at Vera Wang was a watershed moment in her life. She was immediately dressing models and sending them to photo shoots. She was working with "one of a kind" clothes on a daily basis. She got to meet and know Vera Wang. Her entire experience inspired her to believe that nothing is impossible.

Megan says, "The fashion world is beyond everything I could ever imagine, but the world of fashion is also really sad. People in the industry and the whole world they are creating is fake. They are essentially promoting this very thin, high fashion, wealthy woman that isn't real and doesn't exist. This is why women feel insecure and don't feel 'good enough.' The industry creates a false idea of who women are and what they should be. During the days of my internship, when I wasn't busy at my desk, I started working on a brand of fashion that is encouraging to women and who they are meant to be."

Feeling empowered, she went back to Nashville with the desire to get going with her own brand and her own designs. She secured a partner and they started working on a startup company called Revivalist. The dream was to make clothing that empowered women instead of making them feel even more insecure. Unfortunately, the partnership didn't last, and the brand failed due to lack of funding. But Megan learned some valuable lessons. She learned that things could have been done differently to gain full funding for the venture. She learned that it's impossible to make everyone happy. She learned that sometimes it's necessary to be completely willing to fall flat on your face. She has no regrets about her attempt to start Revivalist because it helped her know precisely what she wants to do with her life.

All of this led to her moving to New York City without a job or a permanent place to stay. As Megan says, she had "met herself in New

York City" when she interned there. She knew she wouldn't be happy until she lived out her unique calling in what is commonly known as "the greatest city in the world." So, as she recounts on her blog (eternaloptimistnyc.com), she prepared herself by saving money while working in Nashville, picked a day to leave and landed almost literally in Times Square.

Megan never hesitates to simply be herself. It oozes out of the blog post she wrote about finally finding a job in New York: "My first day in New York was hard, I sobbed on my bathroom floor and prayed, 'Jesus, what did I do? I am so scared, I miss my friends and feel like an idiot because I'm here, and I don't know if you really want me to be here.' And there he spoke to me like he had a year before when he told me it was time to move to New York. He asked me to trust him and put on a brave face while he worked his plan. While I wanted so much to be the kind of person that says, 'Yes, Lord! I trust you!' and throw worry to the wayside, I am a planner and a control freak when it comes to my dreams. I clung to what he said but also reached out to anyone and everyone I knew in the city in hopes of finding direction. One of the people I called was a friend I had met while interning two summers ago who since accepted a job at the same company. It was in church, only a day after sobbing in the bathroom, that I got a text back from my friend saying she'd love to grab drinks and asked if I had a job lined up yet because there was an opening. We texted back and forth, she passed along my résumé and the next day I got an email requesting to interview. The interview went well, I was offered the position, and that Friday I accepted. Reflecting on it now, what a beautiful picture it is of Jesus asking the sad girl on the bathroom floor to have faith."

> **"I AM A PLANNER AND A CONTROL FREAK WHEN IT COMES TO MY DREAMS."**
>
> **- MEGAN PHILLIPS**

The driving force behind many of Megan's life decisions and eventual move to New York was her ability to remain true to herself. Megan has a clear picture of who she is, and it helped her to sort through decisions on schooling, starting and stopping a business, pursuing things that would propel her toward her dreams, and now taking her first baby steps toward her own vision of one day creating her own brand and her own company. There is no one in the world like Megan Phillips, and she knows it, and she embraces it.

The Amazon.com description of Seth Godin's book, *We Are All Weird*, puts it like this:

World of Warcrafters, LARPers, Settlers of Catan? Weird.

Beliebers, Swifties, Directioners? Weirder.

Paleos, vegans, carb loaders, ovolactovegetarians? Pretty weird.

Mets fans, Yankees fans, Bears fans? Definitely weird.

Face it. We're all weird.

So why are companies still trying to build products for the masses?

Why are we still acting like the masses even exist?

Weird is the new normal. And only companies that figure that out have any chance of survival. This book shows you how.

According to Seth's definition, Megan is "weird." And that's a good thing. She wants to build a brand that takes on the sad reality of the fashion industry, trying to mold women into something they are not, and instead empower women to be who they are through their choices in clothing and in style that make them appreciate themselves, feel strong and live lives that are emboldened. That's a *weird* take on fashion in this day and age, don't you think? Don't put it past Megan to make this happen in an incredibly successful fashion (pun intended!).

EMBRACE YOUR WEIRDNESS

So, what about you? Since we are *all* weird (in the best sense of the word), what is *your* weirdness? And how can you capitalize on it to move you toward your goals and passions? There is no better way to learn and discover your "weirdness" than by beginning with the many free, online tools that will help you to know yourself and give you the ability to set a direction for your passions and dreams. For a start, give these a try:

- ▸ Identify your personality type by taking the Myers-Briggs inventory (humanmetrics.com)

- ▸ Learn your strengths by using the Free Strengths Test (freestrengthstest.workuno.com)

- ▸ Delve deeper into your personality by taking the Enneagram inventory (enneagraminstitute.com)

- ▸ Discover why you communicate the way you do and how to communicate better with others by using the DISC inventory (discpersonalitytesting.com)

These inventories will give you an excellent start learning about yourself, who you are, how you function, the ways in which you relate to others, and many other identifying factors. When you discover your "weirdness," you are well on your way to also discovering ways in which that weirdness can be used to fill a niche, start a business, write a blog, create some music, or design some clothing.

Oscar Wilde once said, "Be yourself; everyone else is already taken." That couldn't be more true when it comes to pursuing your passion, chasing your dream, and choosing the creative fork in the road. Your specific personality, gifts, talents, dreams, and desires are what will attract others to become part of your dream and enable you to grow your dream. People love and respect authenticity and are attracted to it. Revel in being yourself and don't be afraid to be weird.

CREATIVE HELP

1 What are five things that make you unique?

2 What gift do you give the world that no one else can?

3 What is the part of "you" that you're too timid to show the world? Does that give you a clue as to what your niche may be?

IF YOU'RE TRULY PASSIONATE ABOUT SOMETHING, YOU'LL DO IT WHETHER YOU GET PAID FOR IT OR NOT.

SEVEN

Passion and Purpose

RYAN WINNEN, DRUMMER AND PAINTER

THE INTERSECTION OF PASSION and purpose is the place where people often discover that they are living a life fully and creatively alive. Ryan Winnen has been living at that intersection for quite some time now. Ryan is the drummer of an up-and-coming Columbia Records band named COIN. On the side he is an accomplished painter who dabbles in a post-Impressionist, modernist style. Ryan says that passion meets purpose "when you realize that what you're doing can affect someone in a positive way, or when you influence someone to take the leap themselves."

At a very young age Ryan discovered that he already had a passion for his drums. Before he even graduated from high school, he knew that he wanted to pursue a career in music. Through sheer determinism he discovered that there was a purpose driving his passion. Born and raised in Cleveland, Ohio, Ryan knew that though it was the home of the Rock and Roll Hall of Fame, the city didn't have the market for the music he was certain he would one day make.

So two weeks after graduating from high school, he moved to Nashville with a couple of friends. He was skipping college and taking the fastest route he knew to a music career. When he got to Nashville, he didn't know a soul except for the two people with whom he arrived. Being an extrovert, Ryan's main goal was to meet as many people as possible, make connections and follow after what he felt was his true purpose in life.

It took a while. He and his roommates lived quite a distance outside of the musical heart of Nashville. He found a job at a clothing store near the city's center, but didn't quite find himself as immersed in the culture as he had hoped. However, one day he met a booking agent who would later become a large part of COIN's story. Though Ryan didn't have a band at the time, his personality won the agent over so much so that the guy told Ryan, "Email me when you play a show in Nashville." Ryan kept the agent's business card and promised himself to do just that, but only when the time was right.

If you've ever been to Nashville, you know that coffee shops are about as ubiquitous as musicians in that city. It never dawned on Ryan that a coffee shop might just be the perfect place for him to meet people, connect with them and create friendships. Finding himself in a desperate financial situation and needing a job, he decided that his former experience in the food service industry might help him with employment, so he began applying at coffee shops. Forty or fifty applications later, a hip and happening coffee shop named Frothy Monkey, right in the center of Nashville's music scene in an area called 12th South, gave Ryan a call, interviewed him and offered him a job.

The job gave him just the influx of musicians, artists and industry people he needed to begin making connections. In addition, his girlfriend at the time was taking classes at Belmont University and happened to overhear two musicians in one of her classes talking about starting a band. It so happened that they needed, of all things, a drummer. The next thing Ryan knew, he was in their dorm room making music that felt magical to every one of them. They immediately said to one another,

"Let's do this again."

Starting a band in Nashville is like selling ice to an Eskimo. It's a very friendly town, but it's very difficult to start a band. Ryan admits that he sometimes got a little too aggressive in telling everyone at the coffee shop about his newfound musical project. He was simply excited to call something his own along with the two new friends he had just made. Winston Churchill said it, and Ryan lived it: "Never, never, never give up." Ryan admits that his stubbornness and work ethic, and doing it all unabashedly, was what made it all succeed.

One show led to another. People started believing in COIN. Ryan used his connections to invite people in the music industry to their gigs, and the other guys invited their friends from college. The band had both industry people and a rabid fan base working for them. The time finally came for Ryan to email the booking agent he had met at the clothing store more than a year earlier. They were playing a sold-out show. The guy came, and in Ryan's words, "It was this crazy moment where we wanted to work together."

Soon after that they acquired a publicist who believed in them, released music online, did a feature with *Interview* magazine, made a music video and found their name on some pretty influential music blogs. One such blog was run by a guy who heard their music, flew to Nashville to take in a live show and immediately said he wanted to manage the group. Before long they were playing shows in New York City, showcasing their talents for labels and found themselves walking into Columbia Records where the A&R rep said, "My interest is real." Those are words that every aspiring band would sell all their instruments and equipment to hear. They closed a deal with Columbia a few months later.

Ryan's current success is so much deeper than just his music. He is passionate about connecting with people and connecting them to others. He loves putting people together who have similar interests or passions. He admits that he could never play his music or do his art without the support of the people around him, or his support of them. For Ryan, passion and purpose come together where connections are shared.

He says, "Passion starts with discovery. You discover what you're passionate about, and then you start doing it. Once you start living it out, it meets purpose when you realize that what you're doing can affect someone in a positive way, or influence them to take the leap themselves. I do what I'm passionate about to give others the motivation to go out and do what they're passionate about. As a result, you hope to attract other people to what you're doing, and create friendships with likeminded people. Passion meets purpose when you see that being an example for others by simply doing what you love can spread like wildfire."

For Ryan that has come to mean that his life has much more purpose than simply being a drummer in a band. He wants to be a voice. He wants to use whatever he learns as he tours with his band or makes art for people to apply not only to his own life's purpose but to the lives of others for their benefit. With that in mind as he tours with COIN, it's Ryan's plan to meet as many high-school-aged kids who are right at the point of deciding what they want to do with their lives as he can. He plans to take the time to listen to them and hear their stories. Then he's going to tell them that they don't necessarily have to do what's expected of them. He's going to tell them that they shouldn't be afraid to try. He's going to tell them that it's OK to be afraid of failure because every successful person has failed at one point or another. He's going to simply encourage them to do the things that they want to do, in the way that only they can. He wants to be a voice. Ryan's passion is meeting his purpose, and he is influencing for the better the young lives he is touching.

"PASSION STARTS WITH DISCOVERY."

- RYAN WINNEN

A SIMPLE TOOL TO FIND YOUR PASSION AND PURPOSE

You've probably had someone at some point tell you to pursue your passion and everything will fall into place. Do what you love to do and the money will follow after it. You may have even witnessed somebody do just that. But if you dig beneath the surface, there's much more to finding a successful career or entrepreneurial pursuit than just "pursuing your passion."

Betty Liu writes in an article for *Inc.* that that's bad advice. Plenty of people have "pursued their passion" and found themselves being confronted by dead end after dead end and never being able to attain their dream job, even ending up poor. Instead, she says to create a Venn diagram by drawing three big circles on a piece of paper. In each circle, write a list that corresponds to each of the following questions:

1. What are the things you like to do?
2. What are you good at?
3. What can you do that the market will pay for?

Where those three circles overlap is exactly what you should be doing. Ryan Winnen likes to play the drums and paint. He's good at meeting and connecting people, playing the drums, and painting. The market pays for Ryan to play the drums and paint. Ryan is living life in the place where those three circles overlap.

Liu says, "I'm a fan of lists in general, because they help organize your thoughts. But there's one thing you must do. You have to be completely honest with yourself. You have to write these lists down with the freedom of knowing that nobody, nobody, will be reading it. You can burn this list afterward. You can shred it. You can do whatever to make you feel safe. But I promise you that if you write this list down thinking your parents, spouse, children will see this and laugh, then you'll have done yourself an immense disservice."

Go ahead and do it right now. I'll be waiting right here when you're finished.

NEVER GIVE UP

John Maxwell, one of the foremost authorities on leadership, says that when your passion and your giftedness match, you have found your purpose.

If you're truly passionate about something, you'll do it whether you get paid for it or not. Creative entrepreneurs are passionate about things that drive them. They can't help but do them. So why not make it into a business or career? If you think you're good at something, ask other people for their assessment. Once you have their affirmation, use every spare moment to pursue it.

At this very moment people are running their own creative businesses at the intersection of passion and purpose. They are making money teaching people how to podcast, selling gourmet sea salts, showing athletes how to jump higher, designing swimwear, helping authors hone their writing skills, and even playing drums or producing paintings.

All of these entrepreneurs have, like Ryan, had to get comfortable with people saying no. But take Ryan's advice when he says that "no one can legitimately stop you from doing your art. Only you can make that decision." He says the COIN has had to learn to accept the "no's," understanding that the "no's" always lead to the "yes's." Their rejections have led them to the right people. "All of the rejections in your life," Ryan says, "are doors closing because the right ones have yet to be opened. God will open those doors when the time is right."

Ryan is wise beyond his years when he warns that being a creative sometimes puts people in a lonely place. "You see the whole picture, but other people's eyes are closed to it. You have to work not only harder, but smarter than anyone else." So here's his advice as you look for the intersection of passion and purpose in your own life: "Hold self-discipline in highest regard. If you want to be your own boss, you have to create a schedule and be committed to it. You also have to have a balance between the work that you put in and the time that you take to be away from the work. Get rid of distraction and create order. You can't just wait for the "creative moment." You need to focus on your craft, whatever it may be, and the daily exercise of it. If you do this, your strongest creative flow will follow your lead."

When passion and purpose meet, hard work is sure to follow. And it will be successful when passion and purpose meet discipline. Never, never, never give up.

CREATIVE HELP

1 What have your failures taught you?

2 Create your "Passion and Purpose" Venn diagram.

3 What do other people tell you you're good at?

ART THAT LOVES PEOPLE CAN BE AS
SIMPLE AS BUILDING A MOUND OF SNOW
AND LETTING PEOPLE SLIDE DOWN.

EIGHT

Love People

JUDSON COLLIER, GRAPHIC DESIGNER

JUDSON COLLIER IS A designer whose distinctive creations jump off the page, screen, t-shirt, or whatever medium he chooses to use. He can hardly believe that he gets to sit at his computer and create beautiful stuff all day. One of the reasons he gets to do that is because he knows that a key to pursuing his passion and chasing his dream is to love and care for people. Judson thoughtfully describes the essence of his one-man business: "Work hard and be kind to people. I work my hardest not to be a good networker but to be a good friend. Focus less on business relationships and focus more on being good friends. Some of the projects I've taken on have created my best friends."

Judson's journey into the creative field of graphic design was filled with interesting and unexpected twists and turns that, as he looks back on it, involved loving and caring for people. He grew up in a creative family. His mom was a singer in their church, his sister was a talented pianist, and he found himself stuck trying to figure out in what way he was creative. First he tried piano and violin lessons. He couldn't get either of them to stick. While he was still pretty young he got into computers, moved toward photography and videos and started playing around with different ideas using all of those mediums.

He made his way to college pursuing these gifts, and eventually landed an internship at Charity: Water in New York City. Charity: Water says that 748 million people in the world don't have clean water. Some have to carry 80 pounds of water from a clean source back to their homes. Others have to dig in sand for water. Many have to line up and wait eight hours at a well just to get their supply of water. Charity: Water is all about loving people and providing help for them.

Interning there was one of the sparks Judson needed to recognize that loving people through his work was something he really wanted to do. And he wanted to use his gifts to do it. So he did everything he could to develop those gifts. Along the way he was introduced to the photography of Jeremy Cowart. Judson's work with Charity: Water instilled in him the desire to create work that expressed love for people, but he wanted to do it closer to home. He set for himself the goal of landing an internship with Jeremy Cowart. So, on his own, he built Cowart a web site to try to convince the photographer to hire him as design intern. Cowart took one look at what Judson had done and instantly offered him an internship.

Within twenty-four hours Judson withdrew from school and tried to figure out how to move to Nashville and take on the internship. What was supposed to be a three-month internship ended up being six or seven months. He did everything he could to soak up knowledge from the master photographer. One look at Jeremy Cowart's web site makes it easy to see Judson's desire to make a love for people a core component of his work.

Cowart recounts how he responded to the devastating earthquake in Haiti that took place in 2010. He created a "Voices of Haiti" photo essay. In it, Cowart photographed people of Haiti who had written their own thoughts and prayers on rubble they found following the earthquake. Cowart's web site says, "This project was displayed prominently at the entrance of a very important gathering of world leaders at the United Nations in March of 2010. They were meeting to discuss the rebuild of Haiti and they ended up pledging ten billion dollars to the effort. On that day, Jeremy's 'Voices of Haiti' project proved that art can help change the world."

Loving people is in Cowart's DNA. In August of 2011 he "traveled to Rwanda with filmmaker Laura Waters Hinson to document survivors and perpetrators of genocide who have reconciled and are living life together peacefully in the same community. Inspired by the 'Voices of Haiti' photo essay, the portraits in this series captured genocide survivors standing with their families' killers, whom they've now forgiven. Many of the portraits were captured at the scene of the crime to help display the power of true forgiveness."

The congregation I serve participated in an event that is also the brainchild of Jeremy Cowart. Once again, it's an event that is based on the desire to love, help and serve people. It's an event called Help-Portrait that now takes place around the world every December. Photographers use their time, equipment and expertise to give back to those less fortunate. At the event people have their photos taken and are able to leave that day with a professional photo of their own. Many of the people served are homeless, unemployed or even former prisoners, some of whom have never had their photograph taken in their entire lives. One recipient recounts how the only other time his photograph was taken was for a mug shot. Google the trailer video of the event, and I dare you not to shed tears as you watch it.

"WORK HARD AND BE KIND TO PEOPLE."

- JUDSON COLLIER

Judson is very realistic as he reflects on his work and shows how loving people through his art came from a place of inexperience. He says, "I love design from an art perspective. I thought I would be an artist that had some kind of message to give. But I realized I don't have that much to say as a young person trying to take in as much as I can. Design has helped me realize I can empower other people's messages in a way they can't without me, and I find a lot of joy from that. There are so many interesting companies that are desperate for someone to help them communicate better. I'm able to shape their message in a way that people understand." Young or old, there is a way for you to love people in the pursuing of your passion. No matter your vocation, you can add great value to your "product" through your genuine love of people. But it must be genuine. You can't fake it.

A MAN NAMED JOHN

John certainly doesn't fake it. One day as I was spending some time writing at a cabin in the North Carolina mountains I was taking a walk and ran into a man I'll call John, a guy who loves people in his own unique way. During the summer John runs a landscaping business. But in the winter John gets to pursue his real passion. He's a lifelong skier who loves the snowy mountains and who spent significant time as a member of the ski patrol. But he's had to give that up to run his own "snow tubing" business during the winter.

John's eyes light up as he speaks about his business. He loves piling up the snow, getting the tubes ready and providing a great time for all the people who enjoy the fruits of his labors. But the thing John really loves about his business is the opportunity he gets to love people through it. He regaled me with story after story about various people who come to hop on a tube and fly down a snow-covered hill. His favorite stories are those about people with special needs who come for a day of fun. There's a nearby group home for adults with autism and various other cognitive disabilities. Each year the caregivers at the home bring the residents to John's tubing hill.

One of the residents is a young man who waits all year to get out on the hill. He puts on his leather bombardier hat, ear flaps down, fastened under his chin, comes running up the hill and says to John, "I'm gonna be Superman!" So John gives him a tube, he lies down on it face first, spreads out his arms, and goes flying down the hill yelling, "I'm

Suuuuuuuperman!" John absolutely loves giving the people of the home who spend most of their days sitting inside, an opportunity to have a day filled with exuberance and joy.

You can really tell that John loves the people he gets to serve through his business as he recounts the time a paralyzed sixteen-year-old girl came to the hill along with her family. The previous summer she had broken her neck as she dove into shallow water. Up to that point she had been a world-class surfer. Now, it seemed, that was all but a distant memory. As the girl's siblings were having fun taking their turns sliding down the hill, John could see the longing in the girl's eyes. So he asked her parents if it might be OK for her to have a few jaunts down the hill. John assured them that he would be right beside her and would bring her right back up the hill. They agreed to allow her to do it. So John put her on a tube, got onto a tube right beside her, and held onto her tube as they began the glorious descent down the hill. John couldn't believe the joy he saw on her face as she flew down the hill, forgetting her troubles for a few fleeting moments.

Art that loves people can be as simple as building a mound of snow and letting people slide down. John's art is shown in the way he loves people by doing something *he* loves. He gets to meet people from all over the United States and provides for them something they may not be able to do at home. But more than that, he delivers special, personal service that goes above and beyond to make his guests feel special, welcome and loved.

Loving and caring for people brings purpose to your passions and dreams. We are created to be in community. We are made to serve. When you work with and for people you care about, there is a certain kind of fulfillment that can't be paralleled. Making other people feel loved and empowered goes a long way toward creating a dream that will perpetuate itself as people communicate your personal passion for them.

How can you show better love to people as you pursue your passion or chase your dream? It's impossible to be fully and creatively alive in a bubble, all by yourself. Your love for your clients or those you serve can't be fake. It has to be genuine. People can detect insincerity as quickly as sugar-coated words come out of your mouth. Don't "love" people just to get ahead in business. It doesn't work that way. Your love of people, when sincere, will have the fringe benefit of better business and more creativity. But isn't it worth loving people simply for the sake of loving them, and for making the world a better place? Genuine love of people comes from the empathy that's built into your soul. Don't be afraid to let it out, show it, and give people the thing everyone needs: love. Your art will stand apart from the cutthroats of the world when you follow your heart to the place where people feel loved.

CREATIVE HELP

1 What's the most natural way that you express love for people?

2 When was the last time you expressed love through your work? How did it make you feel? How can you replicate it?

3 How can you be more intentional about loving the people around you?

YOUR HELP WILL MORE THAN LIKELY MEAN
FAR MORE THAN YOU WILL EVER KNOW.

NINE

Help People

EMILY HOWARD, JEWELRY DESIGNER

BE NICE. THE WORLD has plenty of hard-nosed business people who couldn't care less about anything else but their own bottom line. You will be set apart when part of your business plan, dream, or passion is helping and serving other people. That's the foundation of the jewelry business Emily Howard started a couple of years ago. Consider the Wldflwrs jewelry (considerthewldflwrs.com) is elegant, simple and has grown wildly popular through the use of social media marketing (mainly Instagram).

Emily started the business after first pursuing music, but discovering that it wasn't necessarily what she wanted to do for a living. As she contemplated what was next, she realized that she always wanted to do something fun, but also something that gave back to the community. So she began building a résumé that she hoped would eventually help her land a job at a place like Tom's Shoes, or Warby Parker, or fashionABLE, all companies that give back in some way, shape or form. When a pair of Tom's Shoes is bought, another is given to someone in a third-world country. Warby Parker gives away pairs of glasses to those in need. FashionABLE helps create sustainable businesses for African people

When Emily set aside her music, she had to figure out how to make some extra money. So she drew upon something that she realized had always been a passion for her. Emily's grandmother had instilled in her a love for making things with her hands. Her grandmother would make jewelry, ornaments and dolls, and would often include Emily in these projects. In fact, as she grew up, Emily always had a "craft room" in her home. She would find herself in that room most every weekend making things.

Now she found herself at a junction in life, going back to her handcrafted roots, and starting to work with metal. It was something she had never done until she discovered that she could fix her own jewelry. She taught herself how to be a metalsmith, built a web site, and started posting pictures on Instagram. Before she knew it people were buying the things she made and loving the way the creatively packaged pieces came to them in the mail.

But there was always more to it for Emily than just making money. She has always been passionate about people and their stories. That's why she wanted to start something that was different and would actually help people. Her part-time job at a cosmetics store was an eye-opening experience. She would always have teenaged customers asking for layers and layers of makeup, revealing to Emily their sense of worthlessness, and their desire to buy makeup to "cover up" that lack of self-worth. Sometimes their mothers would even come in and say, "She needs makeup."

She knew that when she started her own business, she wanted there to be a component that would help people. So she set out to have a voice that people are listening to, whether it be those younger girls, or the "materialistic world," or the fashion world, to let people realize that there's more to the story than just buying something pretty or superficially covering over flaws with makeup. A part of that is telling other people's stories so that customers can see the benefit of looking beyond themselves and helping others.

The mission of Consider the Wldflwrs is: "Discovering wild beauty and encouraging thirsty hearts." So Emily began searching for organizations she could help that would encourage those thirsty hearts. The first organization on her radar was Victory of Heart, a discipleship program in Texas that organized a community of girls to get together and disciple one another in the Christian faith. When that group got other funding, Emily went after a cause that was even more near and dear to her.

In her own mission trips to Honduras she decided that she wanted to help people there living in extreme poverty. Now 10% of each online sale from Consider The Wldflwrs jewelry helps provide supplies to craftswomen on the mountain of San Matias in Honduras. These women are being trained to knit, sew and make jewelry, develop their own web sites, and, as a result, support their families.

Emily has become so passionate about this that she actually goes to Honduras a couple of times a year to work with the women who are beginning to tap into their own creativity. They can now be proud of something they have made with their own hands. They are discovering a concrete way to help their family.

By helping others, Emily has helped herself as well. She has recently collaborated with Nashville singer-songwriters and bands who want to sell uniquely designed jewelry at their merchandise tables. Not only does it help the artists, it is also a big marketing opportunity for Consider the Wldflwrs.

HELPING OTHERS IS A KEY

Helping other people goes beyond those you can help outside of the business. There is always room to create an environment in the workplace that helps the people there, too. Emily finds herself more creative when she works together in a team. Running a jewelry business means always having to come up with new ideas. She says that most of her new ideas come out of team meetings. She recently hired a Director of Communications, in addition to a business manager, interns and social media experts. The team helps one another with issues, problems, or challenges that come about on a daily basis. They work through getting plans into place, setting goals, and managing the business. It's truly a collaborative effort.

Writer Jeff Goins is adamant that helping other people is a key to making connections and moving ahead. He says, "If I see someone with a need that I can meet, I help that person. I may offer my advice or writing services or just my time. I may give away a great idea or connect two people who need to know each other." He goes on, "I try to do more than is expected, to go the extra mile. And for some reason, this surprises people."

Brandon Stanton, the photographer behind the Humans of New York web site, has used his platform to help people he has discovered in his daily work taking portraits of people. One such windfall of assistance began when Brandon took a photograph of a student named Vidal who attended Mott Hall Bridges Academy in a crime-riddled section of New York. In the quote that accompanied his photo, Vidal said that the person who inspired him the most was his principal, Nadia Lopez. Vidal said, "When we get in trouble, she doesn't suspend us. She calls us to her office and explains to us how society was built down around us. And she tells us that each time somebody fails out of school, a new jail cell gets built. And one time she made every student stand up, one at a time, and she told each one of us that we matter."

"IF I SEE SOMEONE WITH A NEED THAT I CAN MEET, I HELP THAT PERSON."

- JEFF GOINS

The post went viral and pretty soon Stanton was photographing all the teachers in the school and sharing inspirational quotes from each of them. The series became one of Humans of New York's most popular ever. Stanton couldn't simply just leave it as he found it. He wanted to use his massive platform to help.

So he started a crowdfunding campaign to start a scholarship fund for students from Hall Bridges Academy to visit Harvard University and provide summer programming for the school.

HELPING OTHERS IS A WIN-WIN

In a Facebook post, well-known speaker Chris Guillebeau writes: "What if there was one thing you could do to be a better friend, partner or spouse? It's actually pretty easy: to improve any relationship, honor the other person's dreams. Figure out what they want to do, to become, or achieve, and then help them do it. Don't do it for them—it's their dream, after all—but show interest and offer tangible support. How can you do that today?"

Our son, Ben, runs a musical project he calls My Red & Blue (myredandblue.com). Ben works with other musicians all the time, mainly doing cowrites and collaborations. He's still working his way through the ins and outs of the music industry and is trying to find his own way on a daily basis. He's creating networks as one cowrite or recording session leads him to discover and get to know other musicians. My Red & Blue is just starting to gain some limited exposure through connections in the music industry in both Nashville and Los Angeles.

But it's what Ben does aside from his music that I believe will be a major factor in helping his career in the long run. I'm not even sure that Ben knows he's doing it, or that he thinks it will help his own brand or business. It's just a part of who he is as a person. If you follow @myredandblue on Twitter, you will very often see tweets from Ben congratulating a friend on a new song, promoting someone's new EP, encouraging followers to attend another band's concert, or praising a friend for playing on *The Tonight Show* or *Good Morning America*. Almost without any effort at all, Ben is helping people by letting them shine, showing and sharing their work, being genuinely happy for their success and using his own platform in the service of others.

In a tangible way he is helping others with a valuable commodity in this day and age: online exposure and platform. Just think how valuable it is when someone mentions you in a favorable way through social media. It often means more than money. And sometimes it leads to more income. Louisa Wendorff knows just what it's like. According to billboard.com, Taylor Swift tweeted the word "OBSESSED," and shared a link to Wendorff's YouTube mashup of Swift's "Blank Space" and "Style." At the time of Billboard's post the endorsement had been retweeted over 17,000 times. Talk about a boost to your social media specifically, and your career in general. Taylor Swift is one of the most powerful media figures in the world. An endorsement from her can completely change a career, and it has for Wendorff. You may not be Taylor Swift, and your help may not carry the weight that hers does, but your endorsement, praise, or suggestion will go a long way toward helping someone else.

Justin and Adam Fricke are two brothers who embarked on an adventure driving a renovated sprinter van through all fifty states over the course of one year. Both brothers are photographers and adventurers, so as they traveled they photographed the many adventures they encountered. The brothers saved their money so that they could leave their jobs and take on this adventure. But their own savings wouldn't be enough to handle all the logistics and expenses of a year-long road trip. So Justin and Adam decided to try and enlist the help of some partners. They put together a clever video and sent it to clothing companies, sunglass manufacturers, and outfitters, hoping to receive some very real financial aid product support. In the video the brothers promised to promote through social media any company that supported them. A few offers of sunglasses and other products came trickling in. Then came the day when Justin found out that a major clothing company, Merrell, would support the trip not only with significant money up front, but also with a monthly stipend. The front page of Merrell's web site is dominated by the words: "Explore, Escape, Get Away. Gear for the Unknown." Merrell's mission is well exhibited in the adventure the Fricke brothers have undertaken. This partnership is a perfect marriage between Merrell's brand and the Frickes' unique road trip. Merrell is making a name for themselves through the help they have provided for Justin and Adam.

Admittedly, the help Merrell provided could be seen as completely self-serving. But think about the ways in which this partnership is good for both parties. Justin and Adam get the financial support they need, and Merrell gains lifelong fans in both Adam and Justin, a unique kind of promotion for an entire year and a fan base. More than that, Justin and Adam can definitely be seen as young men who are on the rise as media savvy adventurers. As they gain larger platforms, they will always remember what Merrell did for them as they were starting out. For a small amount of money (in the grand scheme of things), Merrell is helping some upstart young adventurers, and it is a win-win for them and the Frickes.

So where are the win-wins in your life and art? What can you do today to start helping someone else. Will you be an "Emily" who provides very real and personal support to women in a foreign country in need of a new lease on life? Will you be a "Ben" who makes it a habit of complimenting and promoting others online? Will you be a "Merrell" who financially helps out someone going on a great adventure? Your help will more than likely mean far more than you will ever know. Help someone today.

CREATIVE HELP

1 What is one way you enjoy helping others?

2 How can you better someone else's life?

3 Where can you spotlight the work, passions or art of other people?

PEOPLE LOVE, FOLLOW, AND
EVEN PURCHASE STORIES.

TEN

Tell a Good Story

EVERYONE LOVES GOOD STORIES. We are drawn to them and fascinated by them. We'd much rather purchase a product or an idea from someone whose story we know than someone dropping their random marketing on us like blanket bombs. There's more to a story than just a product you are trying to sell. Listening to the stories of others and retelling them can become an integral part of one's own passion, dream, or business. People love, follow, and even purchase stories.

PATRICK CHIN, PHOTOGRAPHER

Photographer Patrick Chin's story is pretty fascinating. Years ago Patrick picked up an old camera and started taking photos. It was simply a hobby, something that intrigued him, but something that he never considered as a career option. He loved playing around with photography when he was on trips or out doing something fun. But he never thought he was honing a skill that he might one day use to make a living.

Music was always Patrick's creative outlet. He led worship in churches for many years using his guitar and his voice. A year after moving to Orlando, Florida, and taking a job at a local church he left that position when the church suddenly closed. He moved into a position at a local screen printing company where he could express his creativity in another way.

At about the same time he began to discover and use Instagram. He never really thought of it as a way for him to express his own creativity, but he started following a few other users because he liked their images. When he saw some of the things they were doing with this relatively new social media platform, Patrick decided to give it a more concerted effort. He deleted every photo he had ever posted on Instagram and started to curate something in which he could take some pride.

He started posting only creative photos that had been well thought out. That change in his "Instagram philosophy" began to work. His social media following began to grow. It wasn't long before the folks at the screen printing company began to take notice of Patrick's skill in photography and interest in social media and told him they would buy him a camera and pay him to hone his craft. He had never before used a professional grade digital camera, so he had someone train him to use it. His role at the screen printing shop changed. He was now their full-time marketing person using the trades of photography and social media.

Before long, Patrick's bosses called him in for a meeting. They sat him down and acknowledged what Patrick already knew: If he had his way he'd be taking photos all day every day. They knew that it was a priority for him. They noted that he wasn't quite as passionate about some of the other things he had to do on a daily basis. So they said, "We're going to let you go and do that ... but we'll be your first client." It was like a mother bird pushing her baby out of the nest and saying, "Fly!"

That night when he went home, Patrick told his wife the news. She was just as excited about the opportunity to pursue his dream as he was. They talked about it for nearly an hour and both decided that this was the way to go. By 10:00 that same night he was at a coffee shop redoing his web site and starting his own business. The transitional help he received from the screen printing company sustained him financially as he got his feet on the ground as a photographer.

Although Patrick's story is interesting in and of itself, he now makes a living telling the stories of other people. Patrick says, "I'm passionate about documenting people that do interesting things. Photography has been my way to have an excuse to go see people do the things that they do well. I get to take photos behind the scenes of all these amazing places and take pictures of interesting and creative people. I'm passionate about telling through photographs the stories of people, people who deserve recognition for what they're doing."

Patrick is working his way toward getting into advertising campaigns for well-known brands. "I would love to get to a place where I could show brands' stories, and how awesome the work is that someone is doing." As he gets started in this business, Patrick admits that it's tough to do freelance work when you don't have a large portfolio to demonstrate your abilities. He says, "Good images aren't the only standard by which companies judge. Everyone can afford to buy a nice digital SLR and take a nice photo. You're really selling yourself."

"I'M PASSIONATE ABOUT DOCUMENTING PEOPLE THAT DO INTERESTING THINGS."

- PATRICK CHIN

And that's where two stories come together: the artist's story and the company's story. When you follow Patrick on Instagram, you can see his story take shape. To scroll through his photos is to most definitely see a particular kind of story unfold. It's full of farm-to-table restaurants, coastline adventures, hipster bars and the New York City skyline shot through the window of a boutique hotel. The images are distinctive and unique. He has discovered his photographic eye and uses it to tell a story.

Patrick has already done a shoot for the Everlane men's clothing brand. Before they asked him to do some work for them, they had only really done what might be called "super clean lifestyle" photos or studio photos. What they asked Patrick to do with a friend of his was completely different. The two of them ended up working on a city guide of San Francisco. Everlane gave the two of them clothes and said, "Go explore San Francisco and take photos of each other wearing our clothes." The two of them did it for free, but it was a great foot in the door at Everlane, and a way to show other companies Patrick's knack for telling a story's brand.

WHAT IS A GOOD STORY?

Donald Miller, bestselling author and expert on "story" (storyline.com), says that the basis of any good story is "a character who wants something and overcomes conflict to get it." Patrick Chin is in the middle of telling his story. He wants to be a photographer who provides advertising photos for major brands. He wants photography to be his lifelong occupation. As he writes that story, he has to overcome the obstacle of being a relative unknown, build a respected portfolio and sell himself to those for whom he wants to work. He also has the competing roles of being a family man committed to carving out time for his wife and daughter as he pursues his passion. But balancing these two loyalties is helping Patrick live a better story. His dedication to both career and home will make him stronger and more able to help tell the stories of the brands he hopes to represent.

Another expert on "story," Bobette Buster (bobettebuster.com), says that a good story takes us to a world we've never been to before and allows us to witness a transformation. I have experienced this firsthand. When I receive Patrick Chin's Instagram photos nearly every day, I am more often than not taken into a world I've never been to before. It's a world full of cool hipsters drinking Negroni's and hanging out at boutique hotels in the most cutting edge part of town. When I purchase some dishes from Morgan Williamson's Handmade Pottery studio, I am taken to a world where things are made piece by piece, with care and the eternal Designer is being honored. When I talk to Riley Vasquez, his story fascinates me because he takes me into the world behind the scenes of major concert tours. Who wouldn't love to be a part of that world? Never in my wildest dreams would I imagine myself in the same room with Vera Wang, but Megan Phillips has taken me there and has shown me that everything isn't as glamorous as it appears to the outside world.

Buster also says that a good story sees a character going through a significant transformation. She says that people want to "cherish a character's journey, identify with them, and take them into our lives." Identification very often comes with the character's transformation. Buster says that if you want to tell a good story, talk about the darkest time in a character's life. Then find the moment when that character crosses over a threshold, when they do something they wouldn't have done otherwise. Patrick Chin's darkest moment may have been when he was let go from his steady job, but that moment pushed him to take the scary leap of heading out on his own and making a living through photography.

In one of her lectures, Buster says that every story is about watching someone become fully alive or fully dead. Maybe your story is about your own transformation from death to life, a resurrection of sorts. Maybe these sentences are encouraging you to think about a transformation that's been a long time coming and now you're ready to take the leap. No matter your business, startup or form of art, part of getting your message out is telling your story. When you're honest about all of your failures, about all of the warts, about all of the trouble, you'll be surprised to find the number of people who will identify with you and want to hear the next chapter of the story. So go ahead and live it. Then tell it: through your art, through a blog, through your web site, through any means possible. People need what you have to give. People want to cheer you on. People want to participate in your transformation. People want to feel like they have a stake in it. So let them in. Let them listen. Let them help.

Allison Fallon (allisonfallon.com) is a writer who has become a master at being completely honest in telling her story. Though I have never met her, I feel as though we are friends. Though her target audience seems to be mainly young women, I as an older man resonate with a great deal of her writing simply because it is so honest. When she writes about difficulty having a baby, though I have never had that experience, I can empathize with her because there have been moments in my life when have wanted something so badly I could taste it.

Watch how honest Allison is when she writes a blog post regarding a very difficult problem in her life: "For more than a decade, I struggled with crippling food allergies. I don't know if you've ever been in a position like this—either with chronic pain, or infertility, or migraines, or hormone imbalance, or extra weight that just won't come off—where it's clear there is something 'off' in your body but nobody can figure out exactly what, and so there seems to be no solution and no end to your suffering. But if you have, you know how completely trapping it can feel."

In one paragraph she has drawn me into her story. She goes on to tell of the transformation in her life as she began to recognize that the allergies may have been just as much a psychological issue as they were a physiological issue. The posts on her blog are sometimes so brutally honest that it almost makes me feel uncomfortable reading them. But the thing is, I can't *stop* reading it. I am drawn in. I want to see and be a part of Allison's transformation. I want to see if it might inform some of the problems or issues in my life and help me find transformation through them.

Samuel Beckett, the twentieth-century novelist, playwright and poet, said, "Ever tried, ever failed. No matter. Try again. Try again. Fail better." That's what a good story looks like. It's what good art looks like. It's what a successful business looks like. Use failure as your mode of transformation. Then tell us about it. Telling a good story is key to great art.

CREATIVE HELP

1 Write down the highlights of your personal life story.

2 How can you help other people tell their stories?

3 What do you want, and what conflict are you willing to overcome in order to get it?

DON'T BE SELFISH WITH YOUR DREAM. INVITE
PEOPLE INTO IT FOR IT TO GROW AND FLOURISH.

ELEVEN

Don't Do It Alone

YOUR DREAM WON'T COME alive without the help of other people. Make it a point to meet new people every day. Creativity grows when people work together in teams, when a web of relationships grows. Helping others will mean that they will help you when the time and opportunity are right. Working with others and building relationships often create a win-win for both parties.

LARRY KLOESS, LIVE MUSIC ENTREPRENEUR

"I'm very passionate about people. My approach is that if I'm talking to you, no matter who you are, I want you to feel like the most important person in the room." Those are the words of Larry Kloess, founder of the organization Cause A Scene. Larry's vision with Cause A Scene is to discover new musical artists while at the same time helping other people "discover" them, too. Cause A Scene exists "to explore the wonders of music and champion bands and artists on the rise." So Larry spends his time seeking out new talent from around the country, promoting house shows and secret shows in small non-traditional venues, and raising awareness about the incredible artists that he supports with his whole heart.

Cause A Scene developed its roots when Larry was working in the healthcare industry. He read Donald Miller's book, *A Million Miles in a Thousand Years*, and was hit with the concept of his own story and his own legacy. He decided that he really wanted to do something that his future children could one day be proud of, so he decided to do something built around one of the things he loves most (music) as a way of making a difference in the world. His first foray into his new business was with a band originally out of Texas named Seryn. He listened to their music practically non-stop for months before they came to Nashville to play a show at a local club. When they finally came to town, he went to see them with a few friends. After the show he approached the band and, after getting to know them a bit, asked, "If you're ever back in Nashville, would you play in a living room?" They said, "Yes! We love house shows. We're going to be back in Nashville in a month."

Larry's personal story most certainly contributed to his new business. As a child, he and his family moved every two or three years because his dad worked for various hospitals around the country as a hospital administrator. He didn't mind it all that much, and enjoyed adapting to new environments. It challenged him to find community and purpose every time he moved. So when he finally moved back to Nashville as an adult, he thought it would be a really easy transition. He knew his way around the city, but he soon discovered that he didn't know very many people in town and became pretty lonely. Larry believed that the only way he could find community was if he began to create it, rather than sitting around and waiting for it to show up. So he started inviting people to intimate shows in his living room and making the city of Nashville feel smaller to people as they got to know one another.

In the end, creating community was a boon to his new small business. "I started this as a hobby. I never really approached it initially as a business," he says. "My advice to people trying to start their own business is not to do it on your own. It will wear you out. Don't be selfish with your dream. Invite people into it for it to grow and flourish."

That's what Larry's attempting to do as he contemplates the next steps for his growing business. He'd like to see Cause A Scene in cities all over the country, if not the world. He says, "Community can be everywhere. Not every city has the music scene that Nashville does, but music provides opportunities for people to connect." In Nashville he wants to expand the offerings of Cause A Scene. "I'd like to create events that are part of something bigger than the performance itself. The events might focus not only on music, but other creative offerings like dinners or film screenings. I want Cause A Scene to be a movement that highlights the cultural and creative heartbeat of a city and its people. I want to create events where people are able to get noticed and be appreciated. I think we can make the world a more beautiful place."

One important component of Larry's success has been his faith. He admits that he never does *anything* alone because his relationship with the Lord is the center of his whole business. "He goes before me and goes behind me pushing me forward. He has surrounded me with people who are a constant encouragement to me. There is a much deeper purpose behind our shows and events. I want to get the Gospel out to others. It's not ever overt but it's what motivates me to invite people into a community that feels like home to them. Community is necessary to the Gospel being carried out. It's why Jesus had twelve disciples."

You can hear the passion in his voice as he begins to show how his faith, his commitment, and his dedication bring purpose to what he does. "I want to affect as many lives as possible through beauty and art, especially music. It blurs the lines of the boundaries and walls we all put up around us. It connects people. The business is all about sharing stories that really matter."

It's not surprising at all that as he looks to the future Larry wants to involve other people in the expansion of the business. He's contemplating the idea of using Kickstarter, a crowdsourcing web site, to build and expand. Up to this point he hasn't sought out money from outside investors. But now as the business model comes together, he's looking for people to come alongside him financially and operationally to help carry Cause A Scene forward into the future. He wants to work with bigger artists so that it brings attention to the young, burgeoning artists he supports. He wants to take on some speaking engagements so that others are inspired to chase their dreams. He's going to launch a merchandise arm of the business so that when people wear Cause a Scene clothing, it will show that great art matters and community matters.

"DON'T BE SELFISH WITH YOUR DREAM."

- LARRY KLOESS

When asked about some of the failures or setbacks he's had along the way, Larry admits that these have most often happened when he focuses too much on himself and doesn't let other people help or support him. He grew as an entrepreneur when some of his shows were admittedly duds with low attendance. Larry acknowledges that at the beginning he didn't understand his role as a promoter. He didn't realize that Monday night isn't necessarily the best night to host a show. When these setbacks occurred, Larry was taking on too much himself and failing to delegate to others. "There's a lot of strength in two or three," he says, reminding himself that you can't go it alone. "We make our failures synonymous with catastrophes and sometimes there are little failures along the way that have hurt me more than a show that was a dud. I've failed by not making time for family or not serving others well. I now try very hard to put other people before myself."

In the end, Larry admits that God has put family and friends in his life who remind him of just how much he is loved. "My dream is to involve other people," he says. "I want to one day be a loving husband and a father who's devoted to his kids. If I'm a lousy father and an unfaithful husband with a great company, nothing I've done is worth anything. For me 'living the dream' means to love people well, to have time for them, to have a balance in life where I don't take myself so seriously. I want to take the human beings around me a lot more seriously."

For Larry, an entrepreneurial pursuit has a component that will never show up on the bottom line. It's not about stomping all over other people to get ahead or to use others simply as a way to make dollars. "My mom once asked me: 'If it comes to the point where you one day find yourself laid up in bed hurt or sick, who will take care of you?' My parents would be there, of course. But I hope there would be a line of several hundred people behind them whom I've been able to impact. I don't mean that arrogantly. It's humbling that people care about me, when for most of my life I didn't feel that way. Growing up I mostly felt unnoticed. For me, that's more of a definition of success than anything, what kind of positive impact you've had on those around you."

KEEPING IT IN THE FAMILY

A pastor I know has used the concept of developing a team to plant churches all over the city of Orlando. He's doing it in an unconventional way. He recognized that he wasn't getting any younger, so he began to develop a team that consisted almost exclusively of younger pastors and lay workers. He became the CEO of an organization that has one board, and yet operates four different churches. One of the most unique aspects of his team is that his wife and two sons are part of it. His wife is the headmaster of the school they operate as part of the organization, and the two sons are entrepreneurs and pastors who have begun to blanket all of central Florida with the message of the Gospel.

Some might call it nepotism. But I agree with the pastor. He saw in his own family the gifts, talents, and abilities to do the things that would bring growth and excellence to the entire organization, as well as the churches and school. He knows better than anyone else their strengths and weaknesses. He knows better than anyone else what they could and could not accomplish. It may not work in every family, but in his family there is a commitment and dedication to the mission that may have fallen far short with non-family members. The success he has seen is a direct result of putting the right people in the right place.

Michael Hyatt has done the same thing as he created his platform-building company. A couple of his daughters are intimately involved in the business, as is a son-in-law and those from outside the family whom Michael hand-picked because of their very specific skills. You don't have to dig too deeply to see that, as a result, his business is extremely successful. What started as a one-man operation has grown and expanded to a "dream team" that works hard, has fun, and has seen extraordinary results.

THE ART OF COLLABORATION

Jeff Goins writes in a blog post about the necessity of networking: "Everywhere you turn, there is someone telling you that you ought to network. And they're right. You can't throw the baby out with the bath water. We can't succeed without the help of others. We need each other ... But perhaps, we've been going about it all wrong."

He makes the case that even if you're an introvert, there's a great way to bring along other people who might just be a key piece of your dream, goal, or vision. "I'm shy and hate small talk. I'm not a very good networker. But I've learned a way of doing it that makes me feel like less of a sleaze: I network by doing favors for people."

Seth Godin encourages entrepreneurs and marketers to do just that, to give things away. Your art (whatever it is) can be used as a gift. Be generous. Generosity is a lost concept in our selfish world. You will stand out and people will want to work with you when you are generous, personable, and willing to serve in an unexpected way.

But the benefit really comes when people become more than "connections." The benefit comes when they become trusted advisors, or members of your team, or a key part of your staff. Ideas are generated more easily when you can bounce them off of others. There's a reason why brainstorming has stood the test of time. It works! You may be *able* to brainstorm all by yourself, but you'll get more creative and more effective results if you can do it with other people. You may be *able* to get a great deal of work done on your own, but you'll get much more finished if you can do it in collaboration.

I was once asked to help plan and write the worship service for a youth gathering that would host more than 25,000 kids. To do so I had to collaborate with a group of people a year before the event even took place. As we did this very exciting and invigorating work together, I realized that there were three components to the collaborative creativity that was flowing in the room. In that one room where we worked for about 8 hours, there were people who brought experience, wisdom, and fresh perspective:

> ▶ Experience: Those with experience had been here before. They've worked with others. They've been through numerous gatherings. They knew the right questions to ask and the specific suggestions to make.

> ▶ Wisdom: Those with wisdom knew the proper theological and technical questions to raise and input to make. Wisdom made sure that we would do things decently and in order, in a theologically sound way, while being grounded in the goals we wanted to accomplish.

> ▶ Fresh Perspective: Those with fresh perspective brought new questions, different thoughts and insights that built on the experience and wisdom of the others in the room. They hadn't been through this before, so their insights were enlightening.

In a collaborative process, experience, wisdom, and fresh perspective bring forth a creativity that isn't gimmicky or over the top, presents an end result that is professional, and brings an energy that is original and renewing. The next time you get together to create an event or project, how can you bring these three components together in the same room, with the right people? When you don't do it alone, your work will spring forth and shine.

CREATIVE HELP

1 How can you meet someone new today?

2 Whom in your life already could you ask to hold you accountable and encourage you in your creativity?

3 For whom can you do a favor within the next week?

LEARN TO SAY "NO." OFTEN.

TWELVE

Learn to Say No

WHY SAY NO?

MICHAEL HYATT, ONE OF the most successful platform builders, leadership gurus, and online mentors of our time admits that he has a hard time saying "no." He recounts a painful memory on his blog (michaelhyatt.com): "[A] few weeks ago, an acquaintance—someone I met briefly at a conference—sent me an email. These aren't the exact words, but this is typical of the kinds of requests I now get: 'I read your blog daily and follow you on Twitter. We met briefly after your speech in Dallas. I am going to be in Nashville next week and would really like to meet with you. I am in the middle of a personal crisis and could use your counsel. I know you are busy, but this is really important. It would mean the world if you could make time for me. Could I buy you breakfast, lunch-or just coffee-to pick your brain?' I ended up saying 'yes'-and was kicking myself almost immediately. The lunch meeting ended up being a total waste of time. He didn't come prepared. In fact, when it was all said and done, I had no idea what he really wanted."

Hyatt goes on to state that if we don't get better at saying "no," the following will happen:

1. Other peoples' priorities will take precedence over ours.
2. Mere acquaintances—people we barely know!—will crowd out time with family and close friends.
3. We will not have the time we need for rest and recovery.
4. We will end up frustrated and stressed.
5. We won't be able to say "yes" to the really important things.

He concludes, "This last one was the clincher for me. Every time I say 'no' to something that is not important, I am saying 'yes' to something that is."

Learning to say "no" is one way toward loving yourself and taking charge of the things you need to do to be fully and creatively alive. One downfall of working as an entrepreneur and creating great art is forgetting to take care of yourself. Judson Collier, the designer we met earlier in the book, had to learn the hard way that you have to have balance as a person. At one point he was working fourteen- to sixteen-hour days trying to cover all the work he had taken on. In the midst of all of that he bottomed out and fell asleep for twelve hours, unable to complete one of his projects.

He discovered that he was driven too much by the fear that if he didn't take on a certain project he would lose that client and they would never return to him again. It turns out it was an unfounded fear. He has learned that people are impressed when he says "no" to projects simply because he doesn't have the time. It makes his work more scarce. It sends people the message that what he does is valuable. It gives him the time to really love the clients that he has, producing for them a product that hits precisely their targeted needs. Which, in turn, helps them feel loved as a customer.

TAKING THE GUILT OUT OF SAYING NO

I was once approached by the leader of a regional Christian women's organization to commit to being their chaplain for a three-year period of time. When she asked, I happened to be in the middle of a writing project for a church publisher and just didn't have the time to commit to one more thing. Granted, the writing project wasn't going to take me three years to complete, but I wanted to leave room for future writing projects and opportunities. So I said "no." She pressed me on it, but I remained firm in my resolve, and felt relief that I had done so.

It happens on an institutional level, as well. The congregation I serve was operating under an antiquated system of governance and structure. It meant that every month five different groups would get together to provide vision and leadership for different areas of the church. It sounds good in theory, but the meetings became a waste of time under leadership that wasn't always well trained, and things weren't being accomplished the way they could have or should have been. When we recognized what was—or wasn't—happening, we did away with four of the five committees and instead put activities in the hands of any member of the congregation who had an idea and the wherewithal to accomplish it. We said "no" to something that wasn't effective, and "yes" to a grassroots structure that has brought a renewed energy to our programming.

Camille Preston, founder and CEO of AIM Leadership, helps take away the guilt of saying "no" and gives you the permission to do so in a post she writes for Fortune.com. Among the reasons she gives for saying "no" is that it helps to simplify your commitments. "Resign from boards, committees, organizations or commitments that are not value added. If you don't enjoy it, aren't fulfilled by it, or it doesn't help you personally or professionally, stop doing it. Make sure each commitment is meaningful and worth your time. And 'just for fun' is A-OK in my book."

And here's one that will really make your life more happy and productive: minimize meetings. She says, "Say no to meetings that aren't essential. Do you really need to go? Is it critical for you to be there? Again, weigh it against your goals and responsibilities. If it measures up meaningfully, do it. If not, don't go. And only attend meetings where the creator has planned enough to include the agenda."

It's all about focus. When you know your purpose, set your goals and narrow it all down to the one direction you'd like to go, it becomes much easier to know when to say "no." Saying "no" can be risky, but if you do it properly, you can do it without burning bridges or hurting or offending other people. Brian de Haaff, CEO of Aha!, in an article for Linkedin, says that saying "no" in the proper way can show your respect for others. If you simply ignore a request, he says, you will be showing a clear disrespect.

HOW TO SAY NO

So here's what you *should* do, according to de Haaff: Completely listen to, and take in, a request when it is made. You are showing that the person making the request is valued. As you are listening, get to the heart of the request. Know what is really being asked. Then, know your own goal and vision. When you do, you will know whether a request aligns with where you want to go. After that, respond as quickly as you possibly can. Quickly analyze the request to see if it fits your goals. Then say "yes" or "no." When you do, especially if the answer is a "no," be transparent about *why* you are denying the request. De Haaff concludes by revealing: "Successful people learn how to say 'no' to requests based on a framework that helps them assess value vs. effort. Saying 'no' to more requests is one of the biggest favors you can do for your organization and yourself."

Yaseen Dadabhay, also in an article for Linkedin, reminds us that saying "no" is a skill that must be developed and used. He gives the example of his local video store. The store has come up with a "no late fees" policy to remain competitive with the online streaming companies. A side effect is that people keep the movies, so when someone goes into the store for a specific video, they often find that it has been checked out and the store has no idea when it will be back in stock. It's a great way to lose customers. Dadabhay says, "Now if I were the VP of Marketing for one of their competitors, I'd charge ahead with some sort of 'guaranteed in stock' campaign to begin saying yes to those customers that this store just bailed on."

Dadabhay makes the case that if you want to say "yes" to the things that are most important to you, you will be saying "no" much more often. "When you say no, usually the person who hears it will react negatively, sometimes mildly, sometimes strongly. Don't let that bother you—their reaction has a lot more to do with them than it does with you. If they push you too much, I suggest you simply turn it around on them by emphasizing the no that would accompany the yes. For example, 'Why are you asking me to say no to my business, and so on, just so I can say yes to your request?' If it's not what you truly want, say no."

> **"MAKE SURE EACH COMMITMENT IS MEANINGFUL AND WORTH YOUR TIME."**
>
> **- CAMILLE PRESTON**

Steve Jobs said, "People think focus means saying yes to the thing you've got to focus on. But that's not what it means at all. It means saying no to the hundred other good ideas that there are. You have to pick carefully. I'm actually as proud of the things we haven't done as the things I have done. Innovation is saying 'no' to 1,000 things."

Entrepreneur Magazine teaches how to say "no" with four suggestions. First, identify whether or not an event or opportunity is worthwhile. If it's not relevant to your business or art, say "no." Second, choose your clients with care. Seth Godin often remarks that it's OK to fire a client or customer if there is no way to please her. You have plenty of other raving fans who will support your business or art. Third, say "no" if you can't sell something that someone wants you to give away. Never give away something that can be easily sold. Finally, talk with your existing clients and let them know your needs. Simply let people know what you can and cannot do. Don't be afraid to let people know your limitations.

Learn to say "no." Often. A "no" frequently leads to a "yes." Saying no narrows your focus and allows you to say yes to the things that really matter and advances the pursuit of your passions and dreams. It will make you more productive and, more than likely, much more happy doing the things that make you feel fully and creatively alive.

CREATIVE HELP

1 To what unimportant thing in your life can you say "no"?

2 Which unessential meetings can you skip? Go ahead. You have my permission.

3 Which thing in your life do you need to say "yes" to most?

HOW CAN YOU EXPECT SOMEONE TO PAY YOU
UNLESS YOU KNOW HOW MUCH YOU'RE WORTH?

THIRTEEN

Value What You Do

CADENCE TURPIN, WRITER

CADENCE TURPIN WENT INTO college knowing she was going to use writing as a skill, but never actually envisioned being a writer. She thought she might want to go into sports broadcasting, and she gave it a shot, but realized that it wasn't quite her thing. She really found her passion when she minored in non-profit leadership. It became her desire to work with a company that had a true sense of purpose and worked for a caring cause.

When she got out of college, she had the opportunity to do some contract work for a non-profit organization in Houston where she did a great deal of blogging, social media strategizing, and creating of print materials around a campaign they were running. Since she wasn't able to make enough money, she moved to Atlanta, where she had a friend who was doing consulting for businesses. There she helped with social media strategies and blogging for their brands.

In the midst of all of this she visited Nashville a number of times and really loved the friends she had there. She was drawn to the contagious energy of the people, the creativity, and all the self-starters who were encouraging one another. She couldn't resist moving there and began with a job as a copywriter. It provided valuable experience, but the job bored her to tears. She's a creative soul and the work she was doing wasn't creative in any way. Her boredom was the nudge she needed to begin looking for something about which she could be passionate.

That's when she got a job at the Nashville Rescue Mission. Everything seemed to come together: a non-profit with purpose; an opportunity to write; creating materials through social media that told the story of the Mission; an opportunity to believe that her work was really making a difference. It was another stepping stone to build her value as a writer.

Pretty soon her desire to take another career step toward even more creative freedom drove her further. She wanted to work for a place that allowed her the opportunity to use her personal voice. So, as many passion pursuers do, she took matters into her own hands and began doing some creatively personal work on the side, taking advantage of some freelance opportunities.

That's what eventually drew her to Donald Miller's company, Storyline. Everything she had done up to this point created value that Storyline immediately saw in her. The company was looking for a culture fit, as much as they were looking for a decent copywriter. Cadence fit the bill on both counts. For her it was the avenue she was seeking. She believed in their work and it gave her the way to write personal stories with a creative bent. It was yet another opportunity to drive up her value as she worked under respected mentors.

She started as a part-time writer, but within two weeks the people at Storyline hired her full-time. They recognized her value as a copywriter, editor, and curator of content, someone who could help with scheduling writers and posts, and work personally with contributors to the main Storyline blog. Cadence loved working for Storyline because it fed her need for serendipity and regular variety in her work. She felt fortunate to work for a "startup" company, being able to help them at an almost ground-floor level. She got to voice her ideas and make things happen for the people the company served and she was able to explore creative ideas with her coworkers and make them come to life.

But if you think Cadence was satisfied simply doing her daily 9-to-5 work, you don't know Cadence very well. Before long she took the leap and became a freelance writer. Storyline gave her the platform, confidence, and last big push she needed to venture out on her own as a writer. She has loved having the freedom to help a variety of clients while also dedicating a substantial amount of her time to her own creative ideas.

Not only that, but Cadence has also started her own venture on the side. It's called Common Table. It came to life right after she moved to Nashville. She noticed that there was an underground movement of "supper clubs" around the city. Her idea was to create one that was more approachable and less expensive for people her own age. Since she loves hosting people, she thought this would be a great way to dig into the Nashville community and help welcome people to the city because she felt so welcome when she landed there. Cadence met a chef who had a similar vision, and they began to invite people to these unique gatherings.

Tell me you wouldn't love to join a gathering like Common Table. The concept is simple, yet brilliant. A form is posted online. People sign up for a chance to attend a Common Table gathering. After the deadline they randomly draw ten people from the list. A gourmet meal is prepared by the chef and served by Cadence and friends. Throughout the meal they explain the information behind each course. Another friend mixes drinks. At the end of the dinner they provide live music from one of the many local musicians that reside in Nashville.

For Cadence, it's a celebration of what's already great about Nashville. Common Table often serves people who are new to town and is a huge encouragement to them as they settle down in the city. The end goal is for people to have a memorable experience that will inspire them to gather in their own homes more often and begin to create their own network. Cadence doesn't even mind if she doesn't make any money at all on the venture. It's yet another building block for her to create lasting value for her own personal brand.

Notice that it took time, experience, and intentionality for Cadence to build the value of her art. It didn't just happen overnight. Her own "storyline" has helped her learn that art you would make on your own without pay will bring in paid work. When that happens, Cadence suggests you make sure that you value your work. How can you expect someone to pay you unless you know how much you're worth? Learn how to value your creative work. And teach others to value what you do.

DON'T BE AFRAID TO VALUE YOURSELF

All these stepping stones and all this "real life" experience have given Cadence many possibilities to evaluate her value both as a writer and as an entrepreneur. Her advice to fellow writers trying to make a living through words is that "you really do need to value yourself. Figure out what you need to make to be OK. Don't be afraid to value yourself at that price." The same can be said of anyone trying to make a living on *any* kind of "art."

The way to do it is to jump in feet first doing the work that you love and to create a system of growth for yourself. Cadence says, "Once you've done five projects, you can up your rates." She suggests creating a system that helps a startup worker know when to raise rates, while at the same time feel as though they are growing in their art or craft.

"Don't get in the habit of taking the work that's the easiest to take. It's not worth writing things for people or organizations you can't stand working for. If you're in a pinch and

> ## "DON'T GET IN THE HABIT OF TAKING THE WORK THAT'S THE EASIEST TO TAKE."
>
> - CADENCE TURPIN

you make money, everyone will associate your skill with each project you take, no matter what it is. Put yourself out there for positions that you're interested in. Email companies you're interested in. A lot of companies don't know who to go to for creative resources. Put yourself out there as a front runner for that position. The key to a successful writing career is more about gumption than it is about credentials."

WHY CHARGING FOR YOUR SERVICES IS A NECESSITY

Jeff Goins (goinswriter.com) says that the whole idea of the "starving artist" is a myth. You don't have to starve to be an artist. When you add value to your product through hard work, blogging, social media, online influence, real-world experience, and a bit of dogged dedication, you will find the proper pay for the art that you create.

But Goins makes the excellent point that money ought to be a "means" and not a "master." In other words, he doesn't recommend making art to make more money. Instead, he encourages making money to make more art. He says, "Use business to create meaning in the world and to help that work spread. Don't serve Mammon; let Mammon serve you."

Michael Hyatt takes it a step further: "Making money is not something we should apologize for because of a few freeloaders who feel entitled to get stuff for free." He makes the case that earning money from your art benefits not only you, but it benefits the world, as well. Hyatt is adamant that charging for your work is *essential*. It's nothing to feel guilty about. In fact, it's something you ought to pursue with clarity, integrity, and purpose.

When you charge for your work, it changes your mindset. You go from being an amateur to a pro. More than that, it improves the experience of your customer. People find it difficult to respect what they get for free. They don't necessarily take it seriously. But when they pay for something, they are literally invested in it. They are committed to it. Even more than that, charging for your work has an impact on the world.

Hyatt says, "Charging for your services is a necessity if you are going to support your family. If you don't charge, you won't be doing what you do for long. But even more importantly, making money provides you with the opportunity to share with those in need. The more you make, the bigger impact you can have. In fact, within the bounds of my calling and ethical practice, I believe I have the moral obligation to make as much money as I can. Why? Because there are people in need, and I have the opportunity to help them."

BRINGING VALUE TO OTHERS

Online entrepreneurial coach Marie Forleo (marieforleo.com) has built a multi-million-dollar business with just "a laptop and a dream." Her advice is this: "If you doubt your value as an artist, creative, or entrepreneur, begin with the simple task of writing down three specific ways your work makes a positive impact on others. If you've got more than that, keep going." Go ahead and do it. I'll wait here until you're finished.

Marie says that "really owning your worth and its positive impact on others, especially if you're an artist or creative, is a key part of that equation. Most importantly, owning the value you offer the world creates a powerful ripple effect around you. You do better work, earn more, have more resources to take care of the people and things you care about, and become a living demonstration of what's possible for all of us."

Simply by valuing your own work, you bring value to others. Don't be afraid to charge the appropriate amount, whatever it may be, for the art or idea that is completely unique to you. That's *why* it's valuable. No one else does it just the way you do.

Now what's the first step you can take today to add value to your work? Don't delay. Do it now.

CREATIVE HELP

1 What skill do you have that other people would pay for?

2 In what area of life would you call yourself a professional?

3 If you charged money (or more money) for your skills and art, whom could you help as a result?

DON'T LISTEN TO THE VOICE THAT SAYS,
"YOU'RE TERRIBLE. YOU SHOULD GIVE UP."

FOURTEEN

Resist the Resistance

LIVING IN A DISTRACTING WORLD

I CONSIDER MYSELF TO be a pretty motivated guy. My problem is that occasionally (ahem!) my motivation gets sidetracked by other things. We live in a distracting world, and I live a distracted life. As a pastor, husband, and writer who's trying to stay in shape through bicycling, I find myself pulled in every direction of the wind on an almost daily basis. I've got people to visit, services to plan, planning to do, a bicycle to ride and lots of writing to do.

I write newsletter articles, bulletin announcements, devotions, church email announcements, blog posts, and sermons. As I always say, "Sundays never stop coming." That means I find myself staring at a blank document on a computer screen weekly as I prepare to write a sermon about the text I have studied, the background I have learned, the central theme I have deduced, and the illustrations I think will fit.

Have you ever tried to write something creative, thoughtful, memorable, and faithful every single week? It's no easy task. It takes thorough background study, a unique "take," a free-flowing outline, solid theology, and motivation. Lots of motivation.

A book that I recommend to most anyone who will listen is *The War of Art* by Steven Pressfield. When I first read the book, I discovered something that I had suspected all along. Pressfield puts his finger on something with which I had been battling most of my creative life. He names it for me and describes it for me. The enemy that seems to always be battling my creativity is named Resistance.

Pressfield writes: "Have you ever brought home a treadmill and let it gather dust in the attic? ... Have you ever wanted to be a mother, a doctor, an advocate for the weak and helpless; to run for office, crusade for the planet, campaign for world peace, or to preserve the environment? Late at night have you experienced a vision of the person you might become, the work you could accomplish, the realized being you were meant to be? Are you a writer who doesn't write, a painter who doesn't paint, an entrepreneur who never starts a venture? Then you know what Resistance is."

I'll let you read for yourself Pressfield's remedy to overcoming Resistance. But one of the things in the book that really struck me was the sentence, "No matter what, I will never let Resistance beat me." I am ultra-competitive by nature, and those are "fightin' words." I will never let Resistance beat me.

Yet far too often I almost do. Just about every Friday night my wife and I go out somewhere for dinner. After a difficult week of work we enjoy a relaxing evening trying one of Orlando's awesome restaurants, or gathering with friends, or heading to a local outdoor venue of some kind. We look forward to it all week.

One Friday afternoon I was working on my sermon for the coming Sunday, and it just wasn't flowing. I was having a hard time getting more than three sentences down on the page. It was now almost 4 p.m. and I wasn't getting anywhere. I said to my wife, "Are you ready to go somewhere?" She asked me if my sermon was finished, knowing full well that if I don't get it finished by Friday, I'm a very unhappy and crabby person on Saturday morning.

Tammy told me gently, but firmly, to get my sermon finished. Ah, Resistance. You bitter, bitter enemy. You almost snuck one in there. But when two battle against you, you will never win. Suddenly I had motivation. My sermon seemed to flow. I looked at the clock when I was finished and it was 6:01 p.m. Victory!

My reward? A wonderful evening out with my wife. A free Saturday morning. A sermon that was finished with creativity and textual faithfulness. A message that will be sent out Sunday morning. A partner in the battle against Resistance is a good thing.

THE LAST SHALL BE FIRST

Jesus once said, "The last shall be first, and the first shall be last." I don't think it's what Jesus had in mind, but another book by Steven Pressfield called *Do the Work* also reminded me that "the last shall be first." Pressfield encourages the reader to determine where it is you want to end up with your project, weight loss, book, or whatever, and then plan how you are going to get there. Start at the end and then plot your journey. Set your goal. Get there. Do not pass go. Do not collect $100.

Resistance will get in the way, try to stop you, and do everything It can to keep you from getting to the end goal. But it is your job to keep plowing through. Don't stop. Don't quit. Don't listen to the voices that will most certainly drag you down or keep you from crossing the finish line.

For those who are looking to live a life that is fully and creatively alive, that seems to be to be a great way to start each day. Where do you want to be at the end of the day? What do you want to accomplish? Where do you want to be? Now go get there. It's also a great way to start each year, not with silly resolutions, but with a goal that has in mind where you want to be by the end of the year. (Hint: Michael Hyatt puts out a great tool at the end of every calendar year called "5 Days to Your Best Year Ever.")

When you start with the last, the first will be easy to determine. With that goal in mind the first steps are more obvious and easier to take. At the end of the day, the month or the year you will find yourself right where you always knew you were headed.

The very One who said "the last will be first" is the One who already knew in eternity what the end goal was and had to be. In the manger the end was already in sight. On the morning of Good Friday it was already known what the end would, could, and should be. With his eye on the only goal he came to accomplish, Jesus began with the end in mind and went ahead and accomplished it for the world. The First became last for you.

He was perfect and we, of course, are not. Our nature often keeps us from following through and making it all the way to the ends that are important for life and faith. But he promises to be with you always, even in seeming minutiae. He is there to help you plow through, keep going, and overcome the voices that would overtake. He wants what's best for you. And what is often best for you is to follow through all the way to the end ... to do what needs to be done for your own good, for the good of others, and for the good of the Kingdom.

I challenge you today to make the last first. Where do you want to be at the end of the day today? Get there. Where do you want to go this month? Get there. Where do you want to find yourself at the end of this year? Write down the end, envision what the final scene will look like, and allow yourself to have a taste of the final feast. Now go take the first steps toward getting there.

Don't listen to the voice that says, "You're terrible. You should give up." Use every tool at your disposal to resist the Resistance, push through the trouble, climb the mountains and get the work done. Then, as Seth Godin says, "ship it." Even if it's not perfect, get your work out there. The more you ship the more your art will be refined, and the closer you'll be to that "perfect" ideal you have in your head. In the mean time, those who love and enjoy your art will only see a "product" that they think is pretty incredible from their untrained eyes.

RESISTING PERFECTIONISM

One way the Resistance works is through our perfectionism. Reid Hoffmann, the founder of Linkedin famously said, "If you are not embarrassed by the first version of your product, you've launched too late." I wonder how many projects, songs, books, articles, podcasts and blogs are just lying around in the deep, dark depths of computer hard drives never to see the light of day. I wonder how many of those projects, songs, books, articles, podcasts and blogs would have been enjoyed and appreciated by their intended audience, but the creator felt it wasn't "perfect" enough to ship out into the world. The world is a poorer place because those things haven't shipped. One person's imperfect art is another person's joy and delight.

Recently our son, Ben, was asked to put one of his My Red and Blue songs on a Christmas compilation that the music placement company Sorted Noise was going to curate for Spotify. Ben called for my advice, explaining that it was a song he'd written in about an hour and recorded in about two hours. It wasn't his finest work, and he was leery of putting it out into the world. He didn't want *that* song to be someone's first exposure to My Red and Blue. He was ready to ask Sorted Noise to refrain from placing his song on the compilation, when Josh Collum of Sorted Noise explained to him that this just might be the way someone might discover the rest of My Red and Blue's catalog. It was also an opportunity to get the song into the hands of music placement executives who might be able to get the song on a commercial or a TV show. In the end Ben decided to put the song out there. It's not perfect, but now it's "shipped." After the holiday season the song had been listened to more than half a million times.

The Resistance has all kinds of tools at his disposal. Time wasters are certainly near the top of the list. Jon Acuff (jonacuff.com), a creative author who writes about careers and finding a job that fits your skills and interests, says that we all have time, it's just a matter of what we do with it. He says there's a reason why the average 21-year-old has played 10,000 hours of video games, the average American watches thirty-five hours of TV every week, and American companies lose an estimated $6.5 billion during the 15-week fantasy football season. We seem to find a way to make time for all the distractions in our lives. It's time we found the time for things that matter.

At a book signing event Acuff said that his method for fighting distraction when he writes is to turn off the wifi on his computer, turn on some music without words, and set a timer for sixty minutes. More often than not he finds that when the sixty minutes are over he has made significant progress on his work. Then he gets the reward of going back to a distraction, or two, if he likes.

> **"IF YOU ARE NOT EMBARRASSED BY THE FIRST VERSION OF YOUR PRODUCT, YOU'VE LAUNCHED TOO LATE."**
>
> **- REID HOFFMANN**

Jeff Goins uses the Pomodoro Method. It's a similar tool to fight the Resistance. He says, "The idea is to pick a task and set a timer for 25 minutes. Focus only on this one task. When the timer rings, take a five-minute break, and then do another 25-minute block." Goins puts a familiar face on the Resistance when he writes: "The only thing stopping you from writing is you ... Distract yourself from the distractions and just write." Too often the Resistance looks an awful lot like me.

Though the Resistance is powerful, it is not an invincible enemy. There are plenty of strong tools at *your* disposal to ward it off. Use your courage, your strength, time management, technological tools, even music, and especially good old-fashioned fortitude. Get your art out into the world. We want and need what you have to offer, even if the Resistance wants you to keep it to yourself. Though it may not be perfect, every piece of art you ship will most likely be better than the last. Start now. Then keep going.

CREATIVE HELP

1 Where do you want to end up? How are you going to get there?

2 What is the one thing in your life that delivers the most Resistance, and how can you eliminate it?

3 What can you "ship" tomorrow?

THE NEXT TIME YOU DRIVE BY AN OFFICE
BUILDING, THINK ABOUT ALL THE CREATIVITY
THAT'S PENT UP IN THOSE CORPORATE CUBICLES.

FIFTEEN

Diversify Your Dream

DANIEL ROBINSON, ACCOUNTANT

DANIEL ROBINSON IS A bookkeeping and business kind of guy. He's not really someone you'd think of as the "creative" type. But there was a creative spark deep down inside of him that he couldn't ignore as he sat in his Kansas City corporate cubicle.

"About 2 years into working at my corporate job I felt this restlessness. I wasn't happy. I could see it when I came home from work in the way I was interacting with people. There was this emptiness that I didn't really understand. I quickly figured out that it was because I was doing something that didn't excite me," Daniel recounts. So the not-quite-thirty-year-old heeded the advice of some Nashville friends, quit his corporate job, and moved in with them for five weeks just to clear his head and discover adventure.

That little Nashville adventure led to his working for a business management company in Nashville. The job revolved around a different process, but it ended up being the same old corporate thing. So he went and got a part-time job for Warby Parker, a cutting edge eyeglass retail outlet inside Nashville's über cool Imogene and Willie clothing store. At the same time he began to help his buddy do business management for a successful singer-songwriter. For a few months he did that work for free. Once the songwriter's team realized he was really good at what he did, they brought him on to do paid work, and his business management company was born.

At his corporate job, Daniel remembered thinking that he would never use the skills he was learning there in the cubicle. But now he's using all the skills that he acquired from that and his other jobs to help other people who are on the creative path. Daniel is passionate about interacting with people and helping them. He creatively cares for and loves people by looking at the many moving parts of their work and enabling them to focus on just a few things. His clients include musicians, entrepreneurs, and independent artisans.

You can almost hear the "corporate" Daniel coming out when he says, "Be mindful of what it is you're good at. Hear what people say you're good at. Don't ignore it. People don't just tell you you're good at things when you're not. People have told me 'you're good at this.' That's why I have a little business today."

But don't think for a minute that there isn't a creative side to him as well. Daniel's encouragement to those who feel trapped in a corporate life is to be creative in figuring out what it is you're good at. When you notice that you have some special skills you can start to foster those and press into them. You can do it whether you're coming out of college or if you're forty years into a corporate job.

He says, "If you want to do something on your own, take notice of the skills you have that people will pay you for. In all reality I don't know if three or four years ago I even really wanted to be a business manager. I wanted to be a design guru. But I learned that I'm skilled in this area and people can pay me right now. And out of that has come this really rewarding fun job where I get to work for myself."

Moving out of the corporate life and into his own business has made Daniel happier than he's ever been. He says, "I might not be making the most money, or have a home right now, but I'm more happy than I've ever been in all aspects of life: work, relationships, being active."

As Daniel honed in on the fact that he was gifted and talented at one pretty specific thing, and yet interested in supporting creative pursuits, he was able to diversify his dream by finding a niche he truly loved. It felt for him like the perfect fit. "I can remember sitting at my old job and wondering what it would be like to be outside, work in a coffee shop, get food when I was hungry and not feel pressure about doing so." Now he's able to enjoy his daily work because he took something he is skilled at and uses it in places that fit his outlook on life and his need for creativity within the confines of a pretty structured skill.

> ## "BE MINDFUL OF WHAT IT IS YOU'RE GOOD AT."
> ### - DANIEL ROBINSON

The next time you drive by an office building, think about all the creativity that's pent up in those corporate cubicles. Maybe it's your own. And maybe, just maybe, there's a "Daniel" inside of you waiting to move from corporate to creative and experience a brand-new life.

TANNER OLSON, SPOKEN-WORD AUTHOR AND SPEAKER

Tanner Olson's skill is writing. But not just any writing. He writes spoken-word poetry. What he writes is meant to be said out loud. Tanner is in the middle of discovering where his writing and speaking will lead him, so he's doing his best to diversify his dream. The intent of his spoken-word poetry is very specific: "I want to write, speak and live honest words of love. I want to communicate honestly the things that people don't want to talk about, and I want to do it in a new and relevant kind of way. I want to ask the hard questions and bring up unwanted topics. Even the taboo things ... I want to bring those to light. My goal is to love people where they are, not necessarily trying to change them, but just trying to love them. People are my passion: caring for them, wherever they are, whatever they're going through. And while I do that, I'm learning and discovering new things about myself and my world."

The diversity of methods Tanner is using to fulfill this dream is anything but standard. He has recorded a couple of albums of spoken-word poetry. He writes a blog (writtentospeak.com). He's recorded videos. He's writing a book. He has done speaking engagements at churches, schools, basketball games, coffee shops, homes, and concerts all across America, and even in Germany. For a while his "day job" was being a Program Director at a Christian camp. But even then that part of his day wasn't "wasted." He had all kinds of opportunities to share his spoken-word poetry with the kids he served during those summers, and even with the staff with whom he worked. In fact, much of what he did in his day job was fodder for his creative outlet.

Tanner knew that he wouldn't be a camp Program Director forever, so he kept creating content. He was intentional about making connections with people who would help advance his creative career and he did what he could to advance his dream through all of that diversity. "I want to take the things that I'm passionate about and share those with as many people as possible. I want to help and care for people. I don't need to have a huge house or drive the nicest car. I want to help the people around me. I want to reach the people going through things that are tough and help them recognize they're not alone. I want them to know that someone recognizes their pain is real. I want them to know that they have somebody who cares."

Tanner's dream isn't being fulfilled all at once or overnight. In fact, he's doing his best to remain patient as his passion diversifies. But there comes a time when every dreamer has to take the leap. After a great deal of thought Tanner quit his job at the camp and moved to Nashville. He went without a place to live, without a job, and without a solid plan. But he knew that Nashville, full of creative people, would be the incubator his creative career needed.

Tanner's advice to others is the advice he gives himself: 1. Take your time; 2. Don't compare. He says that comparison is useless. It will just break down your confidence. "My failure has been comparing myself to others like Levi the Poet and Jefferson Bethke." So his dream is diversified in the way that he seeks an array of advice. "You have to ask questions. Go to others who have done it before. Take advice from people who are freely giving it to you. Don't jump into things. Know why you're doing them."

Tanner certainly knows why he's doing what he's doing. He also has a plan for expanding his dream. He would love to be paid for doing what he's passionate about, but he's ready to keep on doing it even if he isn't. That's the kind of pursuit that money often follows. I won't be one bit surprised to see Tanner being paid handsomely to do what he loves sooner than later. You could even make the argument that he's already a long way down that path.

DIVERSIFY

There are many ways you can make a living with one specific talent. Just diversify. If you're a photographer, shoot weddings and work with musicians, fashion designers and travel magazines. If you're a musician, do cowrites, release your own music, pitch your music for TV or movie placements, sell merchandise, play live and put your music on musicbed. com. If you're a visual artist, create a personal web site to sell your art, pitch it to authors to illustrate their writing, set up a booth at art fairs and teach yourself web design. Diversifying your portfolio will make you a better artist. Your net will be cast farther. There will be more opportunities and more work, which, in the end, will support the kind of art you really want to make.

CREATIVE HELP

1 What skill do you have that you can offer for free to someone and add value to her or his life?

2 Don't be afraid to dream about the new place where your skills could take you.

3 Brainstorm the various ways you could get your art, skill, or work out into the world.

ALLOW YOURSELF THE OPPORTUNITY TO LET
YOUR DREAMS GROW AS THE SHIFTING HAPPENS.

SIXTEEN

It's OK to Shift Your Dream

RYAN WILCOX, COFFEE SHOP OWNER

RYAN WILCOX IS PASSIONATE about being successful. That means his dreams have shifted over the years. He dives deeply into things in search of the success that he can see on the other side of his incredibly hard work. Ryan is now co-owner of Lineage Coffee, a coffee shop and coffee-roasting business in Orlando, Florida. But that isn't at all what he had expected to do with his life.

Ryan grew up differently from most other kids. Since his parents loved boating, every weekend they would leave their Chicago home and head for Door County, Wisconsin, where they would be out on the water. It made it difficult for him to gain or keep friends in his Chicago neighborhood, but Ryan didn't mind. He loved his time every weekend on the boat, on the water, with his family. When the family later moved to Florida they purchased a boat in Daytona and continued the weekly tradition of heading out on the water. Ryan started doing poorly in school because he didn't see the point of it all. His passions were in other areas outside of the classroom that were far more interesting to him.

When he got to high school, the family moved onto a boat full-time and his parents began to homeschool (boatschool?) him. The adventures on the boat got even more fascinating as they took frequent trips to the Florida Keys and the Bahamas. Since the boating life wasn't exactly conducive to making friends, Ryan began to turn his attention to volunteering at Florida wildlife sanctuaries. He worked with bears, tigers, Florida panthers, and rescued big cats of all kinds. He was part of a team that took educational programs on the road. These activities taught him at a very young age how to be professional. Though he loved it, he still didn't have a clear vision as to what he wanted to do with his life.

It just so happened that his attentions, like those of many other kids, turned to video games. He started to obsess over them. He played them all the time, learned all the tricks, set up games online, and did everything he could to feed his obsession. That, along with his father's career in financial software, led to Ryan studying computer science in college. He was fortunate enough to intern at his father's company, and eventually become employed in the financial software business. Though the money was great, he had all kinds of flexibility with his time, and his friends thought he had the best job any of them could have ever imagined, he wasn't passionate about it.

Pretty soon his passions turned again. This time it was rock climbing. He traveled all over the country in search of the perfect venues. He loved the risk and the adventure. On one such trip he found himself in a coffee shop in New York City, right off of Greenwich Village's Washington Square Park. He ordered a cold brew coffee expecting nothing more than what he usually tasted in a cup of coffee. But this was unlike anything he'd ever tasted before. He didn't add any milk or sugar, and yet he couldn't believe how naturally sweet it was. Once again Ryan began to pursue a passion with all of his being. He went home and began to research coffee. He bought the equipment to do coffee "pour overs" at home. He started searching his home city of Orlando for a place that sold craft coffee.

When he couldn't find a place he started ordering coffee from food roasters all across the country. As he continued his deep dive into the coffee world, he discovered a half-finished web site for a coffee roaster in Orlando called Lineage Coffee Roasting. It was an intriguing new business in the Orlando area and Ryan wanted to know more about it. So he called the guy running it and learned that he had bought a coffee roaster and set up a small stand in the parking lot of a local produce retail outlet. Ryan bought a bag of coffee from the guy every couple of weeks. He didn't expect anything more to come of their relationship than that.

"THINGS NOW EXIST BECAUSE I'VE WORKED TO MAKE THEM."

- RYAN WILCOX

In the meantime, Ryan's life seemed to be at a bit of a standstill. He broke up with his girlfriend. He started wasting time going out with friends and doing some partying. He began to realize that his job just wasn't that interesting. One of his friends even encouraged him to get a job at the coffee shop. At the time he didn't think much of it. But it wasn't long before his coffee roasting buddy told him he was going to be opening a shop in a local artisan food market. He said, "I know about coffee, so if you need help I could work with you on Sundays or something."

Opening day came and it was "the most incredible rush" for Ryan as he interacted with customers, made split-second decisions, improvised to get things done and made people happy with their frothy drink of choice. What drew Ryan in was the control he had in each moment and the pure clarity he had in what he was doing. "Plus the insane amount of interaction with people was like crack to me combined with everything else."

What Ryan really loved was being able to build a "system." He had control over how things were going to be done with this new business. The light bulb above his head was shining like a halogen headlight. He started working at the coffee shop a couple of days every week, while still going to school and holding down his old job. But now he knew he could never go back to a desk job. He began to think and strategize about the coffee shop nearly every waking minute.

At the beginning, he was working for free not only because the coffee shop didn't have the money to pay him, but also because he wanted to prove to his potential partner that he could be a key part of this new business. It wasn't long before they had a meeting of the minds and they entered a partnership. They both quit their jobs and began to build the business.

It started as a retail outlet, but the goal from the beginning was to be a roasting company. The coffee bar was crucial to grow the wholesale side of the business. Ryan used every opportunity at the retail shop to talk to customers, telling them how their company could deliver coffee, supply it and train employees how to properly make it.

Ryan's dreams had shifted many times up to this point, but this crucial shift in dreams tested him like none had before. When he decided to leave school and quit his job his parents didn't really get it. He had to do some convincing. Yet as he did so, his dad who achieved business success despite never having graduated from college, began to ask him smart, business-related questions like: What is your partnership like? Why will this business be successful? What's your business plan? His parents were excited but they wanted to make sure that he did it the right way.

Ryan describes the shifting of his dream like this: "I've been a different person throughout the stages of my life so far. Animal sanctuaries used to be my life. I knew all about them. At one time that was the thing I was most passionate about. Before that I was living in a boat and I was into fishing more than anything else. I would fish every hour of the day. For a time it was computer science, and I could have been doing that if the right things would have happened. In two- to five-year periods I do deep dives into things and I'm passionate about them. Right now it's my business because it's an extension of myself. Things now exist because I've worked to make them. I can tell people to take a look at our coffee business and say, 'I made that.' That's my thing. We're doing the best job we can. This is what we're trying to create. I'm passionate about being successful."

SHIFT AS YOU LEARN

One of the lessons Ryan and other entrepreneurs have learned is that dreams and goals shift as you learn more about your art. That's OK. Pursue what you want and what you never thought you would. You might be surprised as things shift and change. But allow yourself the opportunity to let your dreams grow as the shifting happens.

Now that Ryan's dream has come to fruition in his coffee business, he does things that he thinks are done by nearly no one else in the local coffee business. He and his partner travel to the sources of their coffee, places like Colombia and Ecuador. They'd like at least 50% of their coffees to be directly sourced within the next year. They're working hard on that, not even paying themselves for it, knowing that it will pay off because it will give their business legitimacy. They want to have control over what they buy, because it will be the kind of quality coffee that nearly no one else offers. Ryan says that 99% of the coffee drunk in America is simply bad coffee because coffee shops are buying "seconds" and "thirds," the coffee beans that are actually sorted out of the coffee. Ryan and his business want to buy the "firsts" for Lineage Coffee.

As I sat with Ryan one day at his coffee shop, I was drinking a cup of his coffee. I made the remark that I didn't even like coffee, and every time I tried it I thought it was awful. I told him that the only coffee I have ever tasted that I liked was the coffee from Lineage Coffee. He lit up as he reminded me that that was exactly their goal: to roast and provide coffee that was better than anyone else's. It was all because he was willing to shift his dream throughout the course of his life. But no matter what he did, he wanted to do it with excellence.

SHIFTING DREAMS BRING NEW IDEAS

John Lee Dumas, who hosts the entrepreneuronfire.com podcast, is an expert on coming to a place of excellence after shifting his dreams. He served America as an army officer, transitioned into the corporate world, then went on to real estate. It was very difficult for Dumas to find any passion for corporate life or real estate. He began listening to podcasts in his car while he was sitting in traffic heading home from his job. He loved listening to these podcasts, but got frustrated when they would only come out once or twice a week. He didn't have enough to listen to.

As a result, his dream shifted and an idea was born. He decided that he would launch a podcast that would come out seven days a week. Now the "EOFire" podcast does just that, and is the base of a business that takes in a six-figure income every month. Every day Dumas interviews a different entrepreneur, asking them mostly the same questions, but each entrepreneur teaches the listeners lessons through their own mistakes, successes, tools, and ideas. Most every one talks about how their dreams shifted. Now Dumas has income streams not only from his podcast, but from affiliate marketing, online courses, and speaking engagements. Sometimes a shift in a dream brings opportunities that may have never before seemed possible.

ONLY YOU KNOW

The advice Ryan Wilcox gives about shifting your dream includes never taking advice from anyone on the direction your business or pursuit ought to go. Only you and your business partners understand where you want to be and what will work. Sometimes that means shifting your dream in a way outsiders may not understand. They haven't been there as you've tried to make it all work. Don't give up when things get difficult. He says that people often underestimate the friendliness of those who can help. One of the things he saw as he was working every day at the coffee shop was that he could have gotten a different job from someone almost every day. People wanted to help him get a "better" job because he was nice to them.

For Ryan, shifting a dream is very personal: "When I was seventeen years old, I had cardiac issues. It scared me to death. When I was eighteen, I overcame that fear which led me to rock climbing. I wanted to do as much as my body could handle. I had more health issues in my early twenties. That stuff changed me as a person. That underlying concern about my health and the length of my life put things in perspective for me. I went through periods of intense anxiety. My grandfather looked a lot like me and died young from cardiac issues. I guess what I learned from all this is that people get stuck in the tracks of following everything else. People don't pick their head up and look at what they're doing day to day. The whole idea of my mortality made me ask a lot of questions and allowed me to see the beauty in things. I'm struck by the beauty I see every day. Put things into perspective about what you want to be doing and where you want to be going."

Sometimes that means shifting your dream.

CREATIVE HELP

1 Keep your eyes open for inspiration in the everyday things you encounter.

2 Whom can you ask to be your creative mentor?

3 Where can you shift your dream so that your gifts and talents are being used to their fullest potential?

WHEN YOUR ATTITUDE IS AIMED TO A PLACE ABOVE SEA LEVEL, YOU WILL NOT ONLY FIND YOURSELF IN HIGHER PLACES, YOU WILL BRING OTHERS TO THOSE HIGHER PLACES RIGHT ALONG WITH YOU.

SEVENTEEN

Fully and Creatively Alive

THE STORIES YOU HAVE read in this book are evidence of the worthiness of Seth Godin's definition of art: it is a personal gift that changes the recipient. Adopting that definition will allow you to understand that there is always an artistic alternative in life. In its pursuit many discover a life that's fully and creatively alive. Many also discover that they themselves have been changed.

So what does it mean to be fully and creatively alive? It means living a life that's fulfilling, enriching, always growing, doing what you love (most of the time), while loving and helping other people get to a place where they, too, live a life that is fully and creatively alive. Being fully and creatively alive begins with an understanding that the Creator God has created you to be creative. Don't give me any of that "right brain" and "left brain" stuff. (There is most certainly legitimacy to it, but hang with me and see where I'm going with this ...) I've seen engineers and mathematicians who are just as creative with their equations as a painter is with a palette.

Yes, God has created us in different and unique ways. Some are more *naturally* creative in the sense of being artistic in the way most of the world understands art. But when you understand that art is a personal gift that changes the recipient, think about the way in which scientists have created medications that change a hospital patient by bringing her back to health. I had an audio technician change my life for the better when he installed speakers in the ceilings throughout our home and connected it to a whole house audio system. I was changed when I witnessed professional actors who were far better than I could ever hope to be present Shakespeare's most gruesome play, *Titus Andronicus*. I grew an appreciation for Shakespearian language and Shakespearian acting.

But I wasn't the only one who was changed in the process. Our son, Ben, was in seventh grade and happened to be the only child in the production. His life was changed when he saw two of the guys in the cast messing with their guitars backstage. It was at about the same time that he first picked up a guitar, grew to love it, and is now attempting life as a professional musician. Being a part of that production also enabled Ben to find comfort in front of crowds, begin to learn the skill of acting, and pick up the discipline of learning lines, taking direction, and picking up cues.

THERE'S NO ONE LIKE YOU

Those who are fully and creatively alive do something they like, something they enjoy. Every single day John Lee Dumas presents a podcast in which he interviews a different entrepreneur. Not only can you tell that John Lee is enjoying every minute of every interview (while making a six-figure income), but each of his entrepreneurial guests enjoys doing the thing they (at times, finally) discovered they are able to do with the gifts and talents given them. Each of them is simply doing the things they have always known how to do, or have even learned how to do, mainly things that come naturally to them. And they are enjoying their lives while running their own businesses.

Being fully and creatively alive means always learning. The "EOFire" podcast is just one example. Podcasts are nearly limitless, as are online classes, YouTube instruction, TV shows, magazines, and an Amazon.com web site that has more books than you could read in two lifetimes. If you want to learn something in the 21st century, you are pretty much guaranteed to find a way to do so in a relatively inexpensive and sometimes even entertaining way. If you're not learning, you're not growing. And if you're not growing, you're not living a life fully and creatively alive.

The person who's fully and creatively alive chooses an attitude that has a positive impact not only on her own day, but on the demeanor and moods of others. Our daughter, Ashlyn, works for Sea World as a costuming supervisor. After receiving a promotion, and only having the job for a month or so, her boss called her into her office and told her just how much the seamstresses and others who work under her love her as their new boss. She told Ashlyn, "They said you actually talk to them; you say good morning to them; you're smiling when you come to work in the morning. It changes their whole day. They were nervous about who their new boss was going to be, but they absolutely love you." When your attitude is aimed to a place above sea level, you will not only find yourself in higher places, you will bring others to those higher places right along with you.

You are an individual. There is no one else like you. When you're living a life that's fully and creatively alive, you don't pretend you're something you're not. You don't worry about what other people think. You live life as the unique creation that you are.

A member of our congregation lives a life like this. She's a grown woman, married and has a job. But she dresses in wildly bright colors, sometimes wears a huge bow in her hair, is a balloon-animal artist, and absolutely loves Sailor Moon and other

YOU ARE A UNIQUE CREATION.

anime characters. She even took a trip to Japan to get as "up close and personal" with them as she possibly could. I admire her for being honest with herself and being unafraid to show her true, creative colors.

Have you done the Venn diagram yet from the chapter on Passion and Purpose? You know, the one that has you draw three concentric circles with one of the following questions in each one: What are the things you like to do? What are you good at? What can you do that the market will pay for? It's OK. If you haven't done it, now is as good a time as any. I'll wait right here until you go do it. Go ahead ... Right now ...

LOVING AND HELPING

OK, now that you're back you have found the place where your passion and purpose intersect. When you live in that space, you are well on your way to living a life that's fully and creatively alive. You're well on your way to living a life like Blake Mycoskie, the founder of TOMS Shoes. He has a passion for fashionable, reasonably priced shoes; but he has also found purpose in seeing to it that people in third world countries have the shoes they so desperately need. Every time a pair of TOMS Shoes is purchased, another pair is given away to a needy person in a third world country. Mycoskie's passion and purpose came together in such a way that he's had millions of people not only purchase his shoes, but also participate in his annual "One Day Without Shoes" event, where people go barefoot to raise awareness for the many people in the world who do so every single day without the means to purchase a pair of shoes. The movement had such a far-reaching impact that even I participated one year. I was living in Wisconsin at the time, and it was a cold day. So it was an eye-opening experience.

Love goes with the territory of those who are fully and creatively alive. Blake Mycoskie is one example. But another is the owner of a local Chinese restaurant my wife and I have recently frequented. We had only been there a couple of times when she began to recognize us. The woman is one huge smile. You can't take it off her face. She loves her restaurant. She loves the food she serves. But mostly she loves the people who come into her restaurant. And she's not afraid to tell you at least three times that they're open on Christmas Day and New Year's Day. "We'll see you then, *right?!*" she says. We can feel her love the moment we walk in the door. "Good to see you again! You sit right over here!" We have sat in the very same booth every single time we've dined there. And sometimes we're even fortunate enough to have her serve us. You can't fake the love and enthusiasm she has for her customers.

When you're fully and creatively alive, you can't help but help people. We were born to do just that. I firmly believe that God created human beings with the innate desire to help other people. It's what brings fulfillment. It's what makes most any worthwhile job worthwhile. It's what makes a great team. Two people who work with me on a daily basis are helpers. I couldn't do what I do, pastoring a church on a daily basis, without them. James, our Media Relations guy, bends over backwards to help. Not only does he help me create creative content for worship services, our web site and our social media outlets, but he is happy to help anyone who walks in the door or calls on the phone. Carla, our Business Manager, also goes above and beyond the call of duty to help. She often sticks around after hours or comes to church on weekends to do things that she wouldn't necessarily have to do. But she has the desire to help and support. If you're in a creative pursuit, be sure to surround yourself with people who help, and who help in ways by doing things you are not as skilled at. In other words, surround yourself with the people whose strengths are your weaknesses. These people show me that I can't do it alone. Neither can you.

BECOMING PART OF THE STORY

If our favorite Chinese restaurant shows us love, then our favorite local Italian restaurant tells us a story. My wife's happy place is Armando's in Winter Park, Florida. You can find us there at least once a month. Tammy loves the ambience and the outdoor dining options, and we both love the food. But part of the appeal is the "story" of the place. Armando himself was born and raised in Italy, and has told us the story of the way he grew up loving food and learning to cook in his mother's kitchen. Our favorite bartender/waiter at Armando's is Gabriel, who comes from South America. We've learned Gabriel's story, too. How he grew up in the countryside without running water, and made his way to America where he could find a better life for himself and his family. He ended up in the service industry in New York City, then moved to Orlando where prices were cheaper and the weather was better. We know Gabriel and his story so well that we are called by name and get a hearty handshake every time we walk into the place. He even knows how to pronounce my last name correctly! But more than all of that, Armando's has become part of our personal story. We have had dinners there with groups from our church. The first time we met our son's girlfriend, it was at Armando's. In fact, our daughter's rehearsal dinner the night before her wedding was there, too. Whenever we have out-of-town guests, we are sure to take them to Armando's. Armando's is part of our story. How can your business or creative pursuit become part of the story of the people you serve?

YOU ARE VALUABLE AND UNIQUE

The older I get, the more I have learned to say "no." Time is our most precious commodity. It slips away every day. If you're not doing the things that are meaningful to you, that educate you, and that are inside the Venn diagram of your passion and purpose, you are more than likely wasting your time. Say "no," and don't feel guilty about it. You are one person. You have a limited amount of time. It is slipping through your fingers. Do what matters. Go where you are led to go in the journey that's been placed in front of you. Say "yes" to the things that help you reach your goals, and do away with most everything that distracts you or takes you away from them.

If you have followed this path so far, you will find that you are a very valuable person. People will be more than willing to pay for the services, gifts, talents, and creativity you provide. You simply have to resist The Resistance and get to work. Don't let anything stop you. Do a little bit every day. Don't give up. Never stop. Think big. Start small. Keep going. The Resistance will flee from you when you have a goal and a purpose in mind, when you write it down, when you keep it in front of yourself, when you ask others to hold you accountable.

If you do all of this, and find that your direction is turning 180 degrees, follow after it and let it happen. It's kind of like getting married: There isn't just one person in the world you could marry. There are plenty of fish in the sea with whom you would be compatible. But God puts one person or another in your life, and it simply feels right. Lo and behold, you're at the altar pledging to spend the rest of your life together. You are gifted and talented in more than one thing. Don't be afraid to let your dream unfold. It may take you in directions you could have never dreamed or imagined.

If no one's told you before, let me tell you now: You are a unique creation. You have been given gifts, talents, and abilities that have not been given to another person on the face of the earth. Take a chance. Follow your gut. Work hard. Make time (don't waste it.). Be generous. Learn something new every day. Choose a good attitude without fail. Don't be afraid to be yourself. The world needs what you have to give. Be certain that other people in your life never question that they are loved. Help those who need help. Live a better story. Surround yourself with people that fill in the gaps in your life. This is your call to live a life that's fully and creatively alive. Now go do it.

Acknowledgements

THE DREAM OF WRITING and creating a book could never have happened without the help and support of so many wonderful people in my life. I am forever indebted to all of the people you have met in the pages of this book who were so willing to spend time with me and answer my questions. Their stories inspired me as I heard them, and I hope have inspired you as you read them. Allison Fallon and the whole Author Launch team (virtually) coached me through the process and details of writing a book. I will always be grateful that I found Author Launch. My editorial and support team included Brian Fricke, Leah Mitchell, Tanner Olson, and Tim Wesemann. They helped me all along the way with suggestions, encouragement and support. A book doesn't look good without talented designers. I had the best: Megan Phillips who designed the cover and Lindsay Galvin who designed the interior of the book. Mark Zimmermann is the gifted editor who graciously corrected my grammar and pointed out typos. As a writer, affirmation is a gift of grace. Jeff Goins, Kurt Senske and Travis Scholl were kind enough to read pre-publication copies of the book and offer their kind words. Family is the heart of creativity. My mom and dad, Dave and

Beth Eggebrecht, have always been a creative inspiration to me. They have both instilled in me a passion for creativity. My dad literally taught me the basics of being a good writer as I sat at his feet with other students in a college writing course. My family is my most true inspiration. Our children, Ashlyn and Ben, inspire me more than words can say and have been so incredibly supportive as I was writing this book. They cheered me on all along the way. My highest and greatest praise goes to my wife, Tammy, without whom I would never have written one page. She was behind me pushing me when I needed it. She was in front of me encouraging when I needed it. She was next to me loving me when I needed it. Finally, thank you, dear reader, for sticking with me this far and for your interest in creativity. You make the world a better place with your art. Now go do it and ship it. We need what you have to give.

Afterword

I WOULD LOVE TO hear your story. How are you living a life that's fully and creatively alive? Would you be willing to write for my blog or be interviewed on my podcast? If so, please contact me at eggebrecht.tom@gmail.com, on Facebook at www.facebook.com/teggebrecht, on Twitter @renaissanceegg, or at my blog: www.tomeggebrecht.com.